THE REVELATION OF
JOHN
Volume 1
(Chapters 1 to 5)

REVISED EDITION

Translated
with an Introduction and Interpretation
by
WILLIAM BARCLAY

THE WESTMINSTER PRESS
PHILADELPHIA

Revised Edition
Copyright © 1976 William Barclay

First published by The Saint Andrew Press
Edinburgh, Scotland

First Edition, May, 1959

Second Edition, June, 1960

Published by The Westminster Press®
Philadelphia, Pennsylvania

PRINTED IN THE UNITED STATES OF AMERICA

Second Printing, 1977

Library of Congress Cataloging in Publication Data

Bible. N.T. Revelation. English. Barclay. 1976.
  The Revelation of John.

  (The Daily study Bible series. — Rev. ed.)
  1. Bible. N.T. Revelation — Commentaries.
I. Barclay, William, lecturer in the University of
Glasgow. II. Title. III. Series.
BS2823.B37 1976   228'.077   75-37600
ISBN 0-664-21315-4 (v. 1)
ISBN 0-664-24115-8 (v. 1) pbk.

GENERAL INTRODUCTION

The Daily Study Bible series has always had one aim—to convey the results of scholarship to the ordinary reader. A. S. Peake delighted in the saying that he was a "theological middleman", and I would be happy if the same could be said of me in regard to these volumes. And yet the primary aim of the series has never been academic. It could be summed up in the famous words of Richard of Chichester's prayer—to enable men and women "to know Jesus Christ more clearly, to love him more dearly, and to follow him more nearly".

It is all of twenty years since the first volume of *The Daily Study Bible* was published. The series was the brain-child of the late Rev. Andrew McCosh, M.A., S.T.M., the then Secretary and Manager of the Committee on Publications of the Church of Scotland, and of the late Rev. R. G. Macdonald, O.B.E., M.A., D.D., its Convener.

It is a great joy to me to know that all through the years *The Daily Study Bible* has been used at home and abroad, by minister, by missionary, by student and by layman, and that it has been translated into many different languages. Now, after so many printings, it has become necessary to renew the printer's type and the opportunity has been taken to restyle the books, to correct some errors in the text and to remove some references which have become outdated. At the same time, the Biblical quotations within the text have been changed to use the Revised Standard Version, but my own original translation of the New Testament passages has been retained at the beginning of each daily section.

There is one debt which I would be sadly lacking in courtesy if I did not acknowledge. The work of revision and correction has been done entirely by the Rev. James Martin, M.A., B.D., minister of High Carntyne Church, Glasgow. Had it not been for him this task would never have been undertaken, and it is

impossible for me to thank him enough for the selfless toil he
has put into the revision of these books.

It is my prayer that God may continue to use *The Daily
Study Bible* to enable men better to understand His word.

Glasgow   WILLIAM BARCLAY

CONTENTS

	Page
General Introduction	v
Introduction to the Revelation of John	1
God's Revelation to Men (1 : 1–3)	21
The Means of God's Revelation (1 : 1–3) (*contd.*)	23
Servants of God (1 : 1–3) (*contd.*)	24
The Blesseds of God (1 : 1–3) (*contd.*)	26
The Message and its Destination (1 : 4–6)	27
The Blessing and its Source (1 : 4–6) (*contd.*)	29
The Sevenfold Spirit (1 : 4–6) (*contd.*)	30
The Titles of Jesus (1 : 4–6) (*contd.*)	32
What Jesus did for Men (1 : 4–6) (*contd.*)	33
The Coming Glory (1 : 7)	35
The God in Whom we Trust (1 : 8)	37
Through Tribulation to the Kingdom (1 : 9)	39
The Island of Banishment (1 : 9) (*contd.*)	40
In the Spirit on the Lord's Day (1 : 10, 11)	42
The Divine Messenger (1 : 12, 13)	44
The Picture of the Risen Christ (1 : 14–18)	46
The Titles of the Risen Lord (1) (1 : 14–18) (*contd.*)	49
The Titles of the Risen Lord (2) (1 : 14–18) (*contd.*)	50
The Churches and their Angels (1 : 20)	53
The Letter to Ephesus (2 : 1–7)	57
Ephesus, First and Greatest (2 : 1–7)	58
Ephesus, Christ and His Church (2 : 1–7) (*contd.*)	61
Ephesus, When Orthodoxy Costs too Much (2 : 1–7) (*contd.*)	62
Ephesus, The Steps on the Return Journey (2 : 1–7) (*contd.*)	69
Ephesus, A Ruinous Heresy (2 : 1–7) (*contd.*)	66
Ephesus, The Great Reward (2 : 1–7) (*contd.*)	68
The Letter to Smyrna (2 : 8–11)	72
Smyrna, The Crown of Asia (2 : 8–11)	73
Smyrna, Under Trial (2 : 8–11) (*contd.*)	78
Smyrna, The Cause of the Trouble (2 : 8–11) (*contd.*) ...	79
Smyrna, Christ's Claim and Christ's Demand (2 : 8–11) (*contd.*)	81

CONTENTS

viii

	Page
Smyrna, The Promised Reward (2: 8–11) (*contd.*)	82
The Letter to Pergamum (2: 12–17)	86
Pergamum, The Seat of Satan (2: 12–17)	87
Pergamum, An Engagement very Difficult (2: 12–17) (*contd.*)	91
Pergamum, The Doom of Error (2: 12–17) (*contd.*)	92
Pergamum, The Bread of Heaven (2: 12–17) (*contd.*) ...	94
Pergamum, The White Stone and the New Name (2: 12–17) (*contd.*)	95
Pergamum, Re-named by God (2: 12–17) (*contd.*)	98
The Letter to Thyatira (2: 18–29)	100
Thyatira, The Peril of Compromise (2: 18–29)	101
Thyatira, The State of the Church in Thyatira (2: 18–29) (*contd.*)	103
Thyatira, The Source of the Error (2: 18–29) (*contd.*)	104
Thyatira, The Teaching of Jezebel (1) (2: 18–29) (*contd.*) ...	106
Thyatira, The Teaching of Jezebel (2) (2: 18–29) (*contd.*) ...	107
Thyatira, Promises and Threats (2: 18–29) (*contd.*)	109
The Letter to Sardis (3: 1–6)	112
Sardis, Past Splendour and Present Decay (3: 1–6)	113
Sardis, Death in Life (3: 1–6) (*contd.*)	116
Sardis, a Lifeless Church (3: 1–6) (*contd.*)	117
Sardis, Watch! (3: 1–6) (*contd.*)	118
Sardis, The Imperatives of the Risen Lord (3: 1–6) (*contd.*)	120
Sardis, The Faithful Few (3: 1–6) (*contd.*)	121
Sardis, The Threefold Promise (3: 1–6) (*contd.*)	122
The Letter to Philadelphia (3: 7–13)	124
Philadelphia, City of Praise (3: 7–13)	125
Philadelphia, Titles and Claims (3: 7–13) (*contd.*)	127
Philadelphia, The Open Door (3: 7–13) (*contd.*)	128
Philadelphia, Inheritors of the Promise (3: 7–13) (*contd.*)	130
Philadelphia, Those who Keep are Kept (3: 7–13) (*contd.*)	131
Philadelphia, Promise and Warning (3: 7–13) (*contd.*) ...	132
Philadelphia, Many Promises (3: 7–13) (*contd.*)	134
The Letter to Laodicea (3: 14–22)	136
Laodicea, The Church Condemned (3: 14–22)	137
Laodicea, The Claims of Christ (3: 14–22) (*contd.*)	139
Laodicea, Neither One Thing Nor Another (3: 14–22) (*contd.*)	141
Laodicea, The Wealth that is Poverty (3: 14–22) (*contd.*) ...	142
Laodicea, Love's Chastisement (3: 14–22) (*contd.*)	144
Laodicea, The Christ who Knocks (3: 14–22) (*contd.*) ...	146

CONTENTS

Page

This Means You (3: 14–22) *(contd.)* 148
The Opening Heavens and the Opening Door (4: 1) 149
The Throne of God (4: 2, 3) 150
The Twenty-Four Elders (4: 4) 152
Around the Throne (4: 5, 6a) 154
The Four Living Creatures (1) (4: 6b–8) 157
The Four Living Creatures (2) (4: 6b–8) *(contd.)* 158
The Symbolism of the Living Creatures (4: 6b–8) *(contd.)* 160
The Song of Praise (4: 6b–8) *(contd.)* 162
God, The Lord and Creator (4: 9–11) 163
The Roll in the Hand of God (5: 1) 164
God's Book of Destiny (5: 2–4) 166
The Lion of Judah and the Root of David (5: 5) 168
The Lamb (5: 6) 170
Music in Heaven (5: 7–14) 172
The Prayers of the Saints (5: 8) 174
The New Song (5: 9) 175
The Song of the Living Creatures and of the Elders (5: 9, 10) 177
The Song of the Angels (5: 11, 12) 178
The Song of all Creation (5: 13, 14) 180

Further Reading 185

INTRODUCTION TO THE
REVELATION OF JOHN

When a student of the New Testament embarks upon the study of the *Revelation* he feels himself projected into a different world. Here is something quite unlike the rest of the New Testament. Not only is the *Revelation* different; it is also notoriously difficult for a modern mind to understand. The result is that it has sometimes been abandoned as quite unintelligible and it has sometimes become the playground of religious eccentrics, who use it to map out celestial timetables of what is to come or find in it evidence for their own eccentricities. One despairing commentator said that there are as many riddles in the *Revelation* as there are words, and another that the study of the *Revelation* either finds or leaves a man mad.

Luther would have denied the *Revelation* a place in the New Testament. Along with *James, Jude, Second Peter* and *Hebrews* he relegated it to a separate list at the end of his New Testament. He declared that in it there are only images and visions such as are found nowhere else in the Bible. He complained that, notwithstanding the obscurity of his writing, the writer had the boldness to add threats and promises for those who kept or disobeyed his words, unintelligible though they were. In it, said Luther, Christ is neither taught nor acknowledged; and the inspiration of the Holy Spirit is not perceptible in it. Zwingli is equally hostile to the *Revelation*. "With the *Apocalypse*," he writes, "we have no concern, for it is not a biblical book. . . . The *Apocalypse* has no savour of the mouth or the mind of John. I can, if I so will, reject its testimonies." Most voices have stressed the unintelligibility of the *Revelation* and not a few have questioned its right to a place in the New Testament.

On the other hand there are those in every generation who have loved this book. T. S. Kepler quotes the verdict of

Philip Carrington and makes it his own: "In the case of the *Revelation* we are dealing with an artist greater than Stevenson or Coleridge or Bach. St. John has a better sense of the right word than Stevenson; he has a greater command of unearthly supernatural loveliness than Coleridge; he has a richer sense of melody and rhythm and composition than Bach. . . . It is the only masterpiece of pure art in the New Testament. . . . Its fulness and richness and harmonic variety place it far above Greek tragedy."

We shall no doubt find this book difficult and bewildering; but doubtless, too, we shall find it infinitely worthwhile to wrestle with it until it gives us its blessing and opens its riches to us.

APOCALYPTIC LITERATURE

In any study of the *Revelation* we must begin by remembering the basic fact that although unique in the New Testament, it is nonetheless representative of a kind of literature which was the commonest of all between the Old and the New Testaments. The *Revelation* is commonly called the *Apocalypse,* being in Greek *Apokalupsis.* Between the Old and the New Testaments there grew up a great mass of what is called *Apocalyptic literature*, the product of an indestructible Jewish hope.

The Jews could not forget that they were the chosen people of God. To them that involved the certainty that some day they would arrive at world supremacy. In their early history they looked forward to the coming of a king of David's line who would unite the nation and lead them to greatness. There was to come forth a shoot from the stump of Jesse (*Isaiah* 11: 1, 10). God would raise up a righteous branch for David (*Jeremiah* 23: 5). Some day the people would serve David their king (*Jeremiah* 30: 9). David would be their shepherd and their king (*Ezekiel* 34: 23; 37: 24). The booth of David would be repaired (*Amos* 9: 11); out of Bethlehem there would come a ruler who would be great to the ends of the earth (*Micah* 5: 2–4).

But the whole history of Israel gave the lie to these hopes. After the death of Solomon, the kingdom, small enough to begin with, split into two under Rehoboam and Jeroboam and so lost its unity. The northern kingdom, with its capital at Samaria, vanished in the last quarter of the eighth century B.C. before the assault of the Assyrians, never again reappeared in history and is now the lost ten tribes. The southern kingdom, with its capital at Jerusalem, was reduced to slavery and exile by the Babylonians in the early part of the sixth century B.C. It was later the subject state of the Persians, the Greeks and the Romans. History for the Jews was a catalogue of disasters from which it became clear that no human deliverer could rescue them.

THE TWO AGES

Jewish thought stubbornly held to the conviction of the chosenness of the Jews but had to adjust itself to the facts of history. It did so by working out a scheme of history. The Jews divided all time into two ages. There was *this present age,* which is wholly bad and beyond redemption. For it there can be nothing but total destruction. The Jews, therefore, waited for the end of things as they are. There was *the age which is to come* which was to be wholly good, the golden age of God in which would be peace, prosperity and righteousness and God's chosen people would at last be vindicated and receive the place that was theirs by right.

How was this present age to become the age which is to come? The Jews believed that the change could never be brought about by human agency and, therefore, looked for the direct intervention of God. He would come striding on to the stage of history to blast this present world out of existence and bring in his golden time. The day of the coming of God was called *The Day of the Lord* and was to be a terrible time of terror and destruction and judgment which would be the birthpangs of the new age.

All apocalyptic literature deals with these events, the sin of the present age, the terrors of the time between, and the blessings of the time to come. It is entirely composed of dreams and visions of the end. That means that all apocalyptic literature is necessarily cryptic. It is continually attempting to describe the indescribable, to say the unsayable, to paint the unpaintable.

This is further complicated by another fact. It was only natural that these apocalyptic visions should flame the more brightly in the minds of men living under tyranny and oppression. The more some alien power held them down, the more they dreamed of the destruction of that power and of their own vindication. But it would only have worsened the situation, if the oppressing power could have understood these dreams. Such writings would have seemed the works of rebellious revolutionaries. Such books, therefore, were frequently written in code, deliberately couched in language which was unintelligible to the outsider; and there are many cases in which they must remain unintelligible because the key to the code no longer exists. But the more we know about the historical background of such books, the better we can interpret them.

THE REVELATION

All this is the precise picture of our *Revelation*. There are any number of Jewish Apocalypses—*Enoch, The Sibylline Oracles, The Testaments of the Twelve Patriarchs, The Ascension of Isaiah, The Assumption of Moses, The Apocalypse of Baruch, Fourth Ezra*. Our *Revelation* is a Christian Apocalypse. It is the only one in the New Testament, although there were many others which did not gain admission. It is written exactly on the Jewish pattern and follows the basic conception of the two ages. The only difference is that for the day of the Lord it substitutes the coming in power of Jesus Christ. Not only the pattern but the details are the same. The Jewish apocalypses had a standard apparatus of events which were to happen at the last time; these events all have their place in *Revelation*.

Before we go on to outline that pattern of events, another

question arises. Both *apocalyptic* and *prophecy* deal with the events which are to come. What, then, is the difference between them?

APOCALYPTIC AND PROPHECY

The difference between the prophets and the apocalyptists was very real. There were two main differences, one of message and one of method.

(i) The prophet thought in terms of this present world. His message was often a cry for social, economic and political justice; and was always a summons to obey and serve God within this present world. To the prophet it was this world which was to be reformed and in which God's kingdom would come. This has been expressed by saying that the prophet believed in history. He believed that in the events of history God's purpose was being worked out. In one sense the prophet was an optimist, for, however sternly he condemned things as they were, he nonetheless believed that they could be mended, if men would accept the will of God. To the apocalyptist the world was beyond mending. He believed, not in the reformation, but in the dissolution of this present world. He looked forward to the creation of a new world, when this one had been shattered by the avenging wrath of God. In one sense, therefore, the apocalyptist was a pessimist, for he did not believe that things as they were could ever be cured. True, he was quite certain that the golden age would come, but only after this world had been destroyed.

(ii) The prophet's message was spoken; the message of the apocalyptist was always written. Apocalyptic is a literary production. Had it been delivered by word of mouth, men would never have understood it. It is difficult, involved, often unintelligible; it has to be pored over before it can be understood. Further, the prophet always spoke under his own name; all apocalyptic writings—except our New Testament one—are pseudonymous. They are put into the mouths of great ones of the past, like Noah, Enoch, Isaiah, Moses, The Twelve Patriarchs, Ezra and Baruch. There is something pathetic about this. The men who wrote the apocalyptic literature had the feeling that greatness was gone from the earth; they were too self-distrusting to put their names to their works and attributed them to the great figures of the past, thereby seeking to give them an authority greater than their own names could have given. As Jülicher put it: "Apocalyptic is prophecy turned senile."

THE APPARATUS OF APOCALYPTIC

Apocalyptic literature has a pattern; it seeks to describe the things which will happen at the last times and the blessedness which will follow; and the same pictures occur over and over again. It always, so to speak, worked with the same materials; and these materials find their place in our Book of the Revelation.

(i) In apocalyptic literature the Messiah was a divine, pre-existent, otherworldly figure of power and glory, waiting to descend into the world to begin his all-conquering career. He existed in heaven before the creation of the world, before the sun and the stars were made, and he is preserved in the presence of the Almighty (*Enoch* 48: 3, 6; 62: 7; 4 *Ezra* 13: 25, 26). He will come to put down the mighty from their seats, to dethrone the kings of the earth, and to break the teeth of sinners (*Enoch* 42: 2–6; 48: 2–9; 62: 5–9; 69: 26–29). In apocalyptic there was nothing human or gentle about the Messiah; he was a divine figure of avenging power and glory before whom the earth trembled in terror.

(ii) The coming of the Messiah was to be preceded by the return of Elijah who would prepare the way for him (*Malachi* 4: 5, 6). Elijah was to stand upon the hills of Israel, so the Rabbis said, and announce the coming of the Messiah with a voice so great that it would sound from one end of the earth to the other.

(iii) The last terrible times were known as "the travail of the Messiah." The coming of the Messianic age would be like the agony of birth. In the Gospels Jesus is depicted as foretelling the signs of the end and is reported as saying:

"All these things are the beginnings of sorrows" (*Matthew* 24: 8; *Mark* 13: 8). The word for *sorrows* is *ōdinai,* and it literally means *birthpangs.*

(iv) The last days will be a time of terror. Even the mighty men will cry bitterly (*Zephaniah* 1: 14); the inhabitants of the land shall tremble (*Joel* 2: 1); men will be affrighted with fear and will seek some place to hide and will find none (*Enoch* 102: 1, 3).

(v) The last days will be a time when the world will be shattered, a time of cosmic upheaval when the universe, as men know it, will be disintegrated. The stars will be extinguished; the sun will be turned into darkness and the moon into blood (*Isaiah* 13: 10; *Joel* 2: 30, 31; 3: 15). The firmament will crash in ruins; there will be a cataract of raging fire, and creation will become a molten mass (*Sibylline Oracles* 3: 83–89). The seasons will lose their order, and there will be neither night nor dawn (*Sibylline Oracles* 3: 796–806).

(vi) The last days will be a time when human relationships will be destroyed. Hatred and enmity will reign upon the earth. Every man's hand will be against his neighbour (*Zechariah* 14: 13). Brothers will kill each other; parents will murder their own children; from dawn to sunset they shall slay one another (*Enoch* 100: 1, 2). Honour will be turned into shame, and strength into humiliation, and beauty into ugliness. The man of humility will become the man of envy; and passion will hold sway over the man who once was peaceful (2 *Baruch* 48: 31–37).

(vii) The last days will be a time of judgment. God will come like a refiner's fire, and who can endure the day of his coming? (*Malachi* 3: 1–3). It is by the fire and the sword that God will plead with men (*Isaiah* 66: 15, 16). The Son of Man will destroy sinners from the earth (*Enoch* 69: 27), and the smell of brimstone will pervade all things (*Sibylline Oracles* 3: 58–61). The sinners will be burned up as Sodom was long ago (*Jubilees* 36: 10, 11).

(viii) In all these visions the Gentiles have their place, but it is not always the same place.

(*a*) Sometimes the vision is that the Gentiles will be totally destroyed. Babylon will become such a desolation that there will be no place for the wandering Arab to plant his tent among the ruins, no place for the shepherd to graze his sheep; it will be nothing more than a desert inhabited by the beasts (*Isaiah* 13: 19–22). God will tread down the Gentiles in his anger (*Isaiah* 63: 6). The Gentiles will come over in chains to Israel (*Isaiah* 45: 14).

(*b*) Sometimes there is depicted one last gathering of the Gentiles against Jerusalem, and one last battle in which they are destroyed (*Ezekiel* 38: 14–39: 16; *Zechariah* 14: 1–11). The kings of the nations will throw themselves against Jerusalem; they will seek to ravage the shrine of the Holy One; they will place their thrones in a ring round the city, with their infidel people with them; but it will be only for their final destruction (*Sibylline Oracles* 3: 663–672).

(*c*) Sometimes there is the picture of the conversion of the Gentiles through Israel. God has given Israel for a light to the Gentiles, that she may be God's salvation to the ends of the earth (*Isaiah* 49: 6). The isles wait upon God (*Isaiah* 51: 5); the ends of the earth are invited to look to God and be saved (*Isaiah* 45: 20–22). The Son of Man will be a light to the Gentiles (*Enoch* 48: 4, 5). Nations shall come from the ends of the earth to Jerusalem to see the glory of God (*Psalms of Solomon* 17: 34).

Of all the pictures in connection with the Gentiles the commonest is that of the destruction of the Gentiles and the exaltation of Israel.

(ix) In the last days the Jews who have been scattered throughout the earth will be ingathered to the Holy City again. They will come back from Assyria and from Egypt and will worship the Lord in his holy mountain (*Isaiah* 27: 12, 13). The hills will be removed and the valleys will be filled in, and even the trees will gather to give them shade, as they come back (*Baruch* 5: 5–9). Even those who died as exiles in far countries will be brought back.

(x) In the last days the New Jerusalem, which is already

prepared in heaven with God (4 *Ezra* 10: 44–59); 2 *Baruch* 4: 2–6), will come down among men. It will be beautiful beyond compare with foundations of sapphires, and pinnacles of agate, and gates of carbuncles, on borders of pleasant stones (*Isaiah* 54: 12, 13; *Tobit* 13: 16, 17). The glory of the latter house will be greater than the glory of the former (*Haggai* 2: 7–9).

(xi) An essential part of the apocalyptic picture of the last days was the resurrection of the dead. "Many of those who sleep in the dust of the earth shall awake, some to everlasting life, and some to shame and everlasting contempt" (*Daniel* 12: 2, 3). Sheol and the grave will give back that which has been entrusted to them (*Enoch* 51: 1). The scope of the resurrection of the dead varied. Sometimes it was to apply only to the righteous in Israel; sometimes to all Israel; and sometimes to all men everywhere. Whichever form it took, it is true to say that now for the first time we see emerging a strong hope of a life beyond the grave.

(xii) There were differences as to how long the Messianic kingdom was to last. The most natural—and the most usual— view was to think of it as lasting for ever. The kingdom of the saints is an everlasting kingdom (*Daniel* 7: 27). Some believed that the reign of the Messiah would last for four hundred years. They arrived at this figure from a comparison of *Genesis* 15: 13 and *Psalm* 90: 15. In *Genesis* Abraham is told that the period of affliction of the children of Israel will be four hundred years; the psalmist's prayer is that God will make the nation glad according to the days wherein he has afflicted them and the years wherein they have seen evil. In the *Revelation* the view is that there is to be a reign of the saints for a thousand years; then the final battle with the assembled powers of evil; then the golden age of God.

Such were the events which the apocalyptic writers pictured in the last days; and practically all of them find their place in the pictures of the *Revelation*. To complete the picture we may briefly summarize the blessings of the coming age.

THE BLESSINGS OF THE AGE TO COME

(i) The divided kingdom will be united again. The house of Judah will walk again with the house of Israel (*Jeremiah* 3: 18; *Isaiah* 11: 13; *Hosea* 1: 11). The old divisions will be healed and the people of God will be one.

(ii) There will be in the world an amazing fertility. The wilderness will become a field (*Isaiah* 32: 15), it will become like the garden of Eden (*Isaiah* 51: 3); the desert will rejoice and blossom like the crocus (*Isaiah* 35: 1). The earth will yield its fruit ten thousandfold; on each vine will be a thousand branches, on each branch a thousand clusters, in each cluster a thousand grapes, and each grape will give a cor (120 gallons) of wine (2 *Baruch* 29: 5–8). There will be a plenty such as the world has never known and the hungry will rejoice.

(iii) A consistent part of the dream of the new age was that in it all wars would cease. The swords will be beaten into ploughshares and the spears into pruning-hooks (*Isaiah* 2: 4). There will be no sword or battle-din. There will be a common law for all men and a great peace throughout the earth, and king will be friendly with king (*Sibylline Oracles* 3: 751–760).

(iv) One of the loveliest ideas concerning the new age was that in it there would be no more enmity between the beasts or between man and the beasts. The leopard and the kid, the cow and the bear, the lion and the fatling will play and lie down together (*Isaiah* 11: 6–9; 65: 25). There will be a new covenant between man and the beasts of the field (*Hosea* 2: 18). Even a child will be able to play where the poisonous reptiles have their holes and their dens (*Isaiah* 11: 6–9; 2 *Baruch* 73: 6). In all nature there will be a universal reign of friendship in which none will wish to do another any harm.

(v) The coming age will bring the end of weariness, of sorrow and of pain. The people will not sorrow any more (*Jeremiah* 31: 12); everlasting joy will be upon their heads (*Isaiah* 35: 10). There will be no such thing as an untimely death (*Isaiah* 65: 20–22); no man will say: "I am sick" (*Isaiah*

33: 24); death will be swallowed up in victory and God will wipe tears from all faces (*Isaiah* 25: 8). Disease will withdraw; anxiety, anguish and lamentation will pass away; childbirth will have no pain; the reaper will not grow weary and the builder will not be toilworn (2 *Baruch* 73: 2–74: 4). The age to come will be one when what Virgil called "the tears of things" will be no more.

(vi) The age to come will be an age of righteousness. There will be perfect holiness among men. Mankind will be a good generation, living in the fear of the Lord in the days of mercy (*Psalms of Solomon* 17: 28–49; 18: 9, 10).

The *Revelation* is the New Testament representative of all these apocalyptic works which tell of the terrors before the end of time and of the blessings of the age to come; and it uses all the familiar imagery. It may often be difficult and even unintelligible to us, but for the most part it was using pictures and ideas which those who read it would know and understand.

THE AUTHOR OF THE REVELATION

(i) The *Revelation* was written by a man called John. He begins by saying that God sent the visions he is going to relate to his servant John (1: 1). He begins the body of his book by saying that it is from John to the Seven Churches in Asia (1: 4). He speaks of himself as John the brother and companion in tribulation of those to whom he writes (1: 9). "I John," he says, "am he who heard and saw these things" (22: 8).

(ii) This John was a Christian who lived in Asia in the same sphere as the Christians of the Seven Churches. He calls himself the brother of those to whom he writes; and he says he too shares in the tribulations through which they are passing (1: 9).

(iii) He was most probably a Jew of Palestine who had come to Asia Minor late in life. We can deduce that from the kind of Greek he writes. It is vivid, powerful, and pictorial; but from the point of view of grammar it is easily the worst Greek in the New Testament. He makes mistakes which no schoolboy who knew Greek could make. Greek is

certainly not his native language; and it is often clear that he
is writing in Greek and thinking in Hebrew. He is steeped in
the Old Testament. He quotes it or alludes to it 245 times.
These quotations come from about twenty Old Testament
books; his favourites are *Isaiah, Daniel, Ezekiel, Psalms,
Exodus, Jeremiah, Zechariah.* Not only does he know the Old
Testament intimately; he is also familiar with the apocalyptic
books written between the Testaments.

(iv) His claim for himself is that he is a prophet, and it is
on that fact that he rests his right to speak. The command
of the Risen Christ to him is that he must prophesy (10: 11).
It is through the spirit of prophecy that Jesus gives his witness
to the Church (19: 10). God is the God of the holy prophets
and sends his angel to show his servants what is going to
happen in the world (22: 6). The angel speaks to him of his
brothers the prophets (22: 9). His book is characteristically
prophecy or the words of prophecy (22: 7, 10, 18, 19).

It is here that John's authority lies. He does not call himself an apostle, as Paul does when he wishes to underline
his right to speak. He has no "official" or administrative
position in the Church; he is a prophet. He writes what he
sees; and since what he sees comes from God, his word is
faithful and true (1: 11, 19).

When John was writing, the prophets had a very special
place in the Church. He was writing, as we shall see, about A.D.
90. By that time the Church had two kinds of ministry. There
was the local ministry; those engaged in it were settled
permanently in one congregation, the elders, the deacons
and the teachers. And there was the itinerant ministry of those
whose sphere of labour was not confined to any one congregation. In it were the apostles, whose writ ran throughout the
whole Church; and there were the prophets, who were
wandering preachers. The prophets were greatly respected;
to question the words of a true prophet was to sin against
the Holy Spirit, the *Didache* says (11: 7). The accepted order
of service for the celebration of the Eucharist is laid down in
the *Didache,* but at the end comes the sentence: "But allow

the prophets to hold the Eucharist as they will" (10: 7). The prophets were regarded as uniquely the men of God, and John was a prophet.

(v) It is not likely that he was an apostle. Otherwise he would hardly have so stressed the fact that he was a prophet. Further, he speaks of the apostles as if he was looking back on them as the great foundations of the Church. He speaks of the twelve foundations of the wall of the Holy City and then says, "and on them were the twelve names of the twelve apostles of the Lamb" (21: 14). He would scarcely have spoken of the apostles like that if he himself was one of them.

This conclusion is rendered even more likely by the title of the book. In the Authorized and Revised Versions it is called *The Revelation of St. John the Divine*. In the Revised Standard Version and in Moffatt's and in J. B. Phillips' translations *the Divine* is omitted, because it is absent from the majority of the oldest Greek manuscripts; but it does go very far back. The Greek is *theologos* and the word is here used in the sense in which we speak of "the Puritan divines" and means, not John the saintly but John the theologian; and the very addition of that title seems to distinguish this John from the John who was the apostle.

As long ago as A.D. 250 Dionysius, the great scholar who was head of the Christian school at Alexandria, saw that it was well nigh impossible that the same man could have written the *Revelation* and the Fourth Gospel, if for no other reason than that the Greek is so different. The Greek of the Fourth Gospel is simple but correct; the Greek of the *Revelation* is rugged and vivid, but notoriously incorrect. Further, the writer of the Fourth Gospel studiously avoids any mention of his own name; the John of the *Revelation* repeatedly mentions it. Still further, the ideas of the two books are different. The great ideas of the Fourth Gospel, light, life, truth and grace, do not dominate the *Revelation*. At the same time there are enough resemblances in thought and language to make it clear that both books come from the same centre and from the same world of thought.

THE DATE OF THE REVELATION

We have two sources which enable us to fix the date.

(i) There is the account which tradition gives to us. The consistent tradition is that John was banished to Patmos in the time of Domitian; that he saw his visions there; at the death of Domitian was liberated and came back to Ephesus; and there set down the visions he had seen. Victorinus, who wrote towards the end of the third century A.D., says in his commentary on the *Revelation*: "John, when he saw these things, was in the island of Patmos, condemned to the mines by Domitian the Emperor. There, therefore, he saw the revelation ... When he was afterwards set free from the mines, he handed down this revelation which he had received from God." Jerome is even more detailed: "In the fourteenth year after the persecution of Nero, John was banished to the island of Patmos, and there wrote the *Revelation* ... Upon the death of Domitian, and upon the repeal of his acts by the senate, because of their excessive cruelty, he returned to Ephesus, when Nerva was emperor." Eusebius says: "The apostle and evangelist John related these things to the Churches, when he had returned from exile in the island after the death of Domitian." Tradition makes it certain that John saw his visions in exile in Patmos; the only thing that is doubtful—and it is not important—is whether he wrote them down during the time of his banishment or when he returned to Ephesus. On this evidence we will not be wrong if we date the *Revelation* about A.D. 95.

(ii) The second line of evidence is the material in the book. There is a completely new attitude to Rome and to the Roman Empire.

In *Acts* the tribunal of the Roman magistrate was often the safest refuge of the Christian missionaries against the hatred of the Jews and the fury of the mob. Paul was proud that he was a Roman citizen and again and again claimed the rights to which every Roman citizen was entitled. In Philippi he brought the local magistrates to heel by revealing his citizenship (*Acts* 16: 36–40). In Corinth Gallio dismissed the complaints against him with impartial Roman justice (*Acts* 18: 1–17). In Ephesus the Roman authorities were careful for his safety against the rioting mob (*Acts* 19: 13–41). In Jerusalem the Roman tribune rescued him from what might have become a lynching (*Acts* 21: 30–40). When the Roman tribune in Jerusalem heard that there was to be an attempt on Paul's life on the way to Caesarea, he took every possible step to ensure his safety (*Acts* 23: 12–31). When Paul despaired of justice in Palestine, he exercised his right as a citizen and appealed direct to Caesar (*Acts* 25: 10, 11). When he wrote to the Romans, he urged upon them obedience to the powers that be, because they were ordained by God and were a terror only to the evil, and not to the good (*Romans* 13: 1–7). Peter's advice is exactly the same. Governors and kings are to be obeyed, for their task is given them by God. It is a Christian's duty to fear God and honour the emperor (1 *Peter* 2: 12–17). In writing to the Thessalonians it is likely that Paul points to the power of Rome as the one thing which is controlling the threatening chaos of the world (2 *Thessalonians* 2: 7).

In the *Revelation* there is nothing but blazing hatred for Rome. Rome is a Babylon, the mother of harlots, drunk with the blood of the saints and the martyrs (*Revelation* 17: 5, 6). John hopes for nothing but her total destruction.

The explanation of this change in attitude lies in the wide development of Caesar worship which, with its accompanying persecution, is the background of the *Revelation*.

By the time of the *Revelation* Caesar worship was the one religion which covered the whole Roman Empire; and it was because of their refusal to conform to its demands that Christians were persecuted and killed. Its essence was that the reigning Roman Emperor, as embodying the spirit of Rome, was divine. Once a year everyone in the Empire had to appear before the magistrates to burn a pinch of incense to the godhead of Caesar and to say: "Caesar is Lord." After he had done that, a man might go away and worship any god or goddess he liked, so long as that worship did not infringe decency and good order; but he must go through this ceremony in which he acknowledged the Emperor's divinity.

The reason was very simple. Rome had a vast heterogeneous empire, stretching from one end of the known world to another. It had in it many tongues, races and traditions. The problem was how to weld this varied mass into a self-conscious unity. There is no unifying force like that of a common religion but none of the national religions could conceivably have become universal. Caesar worship could. It was the one common act and belief which turned the Empire into a unity. To refuse to burn the pinch of incense and to say: "Caesar is Lord," was not an act of irreligion; it was an act of political disloyalty. That is why the Romans dealt with the utmost severity with the man who would not say: "Caesar is Lord." And no Christian could give the title Lord to any other than Jesus Christ. This was the centre of his creed.

We must see how this Caesar worship developed and how it was at its peak when the *Revelation* was written.

One basic fact must be noted. Caesar worship was not imposed on the people from above. It arose from the people; it might even be said that it arose in spite of efforts by the early emperors to stop it, or at least to curb it. And it is to be noted that of all the people in the Empire only the Jews were exempt from it.

Caesar worship began as a spontaneous outburst of gratitude to Rome. The people of the provinces well knew what they owed to Rome. Impartial Roman justice had taken the place of capricious and tyrannical oppression. Security had taken the place of insecurity. The great Roman roads spanned the world; and the roads were safe from brigands and the seas were clear of pirates. The *pax Romana*, the Roman peace, was the greatest thing which ever happened to the ancient world. As Virgil had it, Rome felt her destiny to be "to spare the fallen and to cast down the proud." Life had a new order about it. E. J. Goodspeed writes: "This was the *pax Romana*. The provincial under Roman sway found himself in a position to conduct his business, provide for his family, send his letters, and make his journeys in security, thanks to the strong hand of Rome."

Caesar worship did not begin with the deification of the Emperor. It began with the deification of Rome. The spirit of the Empire was deified under the name of the goddess Roma. Roma stood for all the strong and benevolent power of the Empire. The first temple to Roma was erected in Smyrna as far back as 195 B.C. It was no great step to think of the spirit of Rome being incarnated in one man, the Emperor. The worship of the Emperor began with the worship of Julius Caesar after his death. In 29 B.C. the Emperor Augustus granted to the provinces of Asia and Bithynia permission to erect temples in Ephesus and Nicaea for the joint worship of the goddess Roma and the deified Julius Caesar. At these shrines Roman citizens were encouraged and even exhorted to worship. Then another step was taken. To provincials who were *not* Roman citizens Augustus gave permission to erect temples in Pergamum in Asia and in Nicomedia in Bithynia, for the worship of Roma and *himself*. At first the worship of the reigning Emperor was considered to be something permissible for provincial non-citizens, but not for those who had the dignity of the citizenship.

There was an inevitable development. It is human to worship a god who can be seen rather than a spirit. Gradually men began more and more to worship the Emperor himself instead of the goddess Roma. It still required special permission from the senate to erect a temple to the living Emperor, but by the middle of the first century that permission was more and more freely given. Caesar worship was becoming the universal religion of the Roman Empire. A priesthood developed and the worship was organized into presbyteries, whose officials were held in the highest honour.

This worship was never intended to wipe out other religions. Rome was essentially tolerant. A man might worship Caesar *and* his own god. But more and more Caesar worship became a test of political loyalty; it became, as has been said, the recognition of the dominion of Caesar over a man's life and soul. Let us, then trace the development of this worship up to, and immediately beyond, the writing of the *Revelation*.

(i) Augustus, who died in A.D. 14, allowed the worship of Julius Caesar, his great predecessor. He allowed non-citizens in the provinces to worship himself but he did not permit citizens to do so; and he made no attempt to enforce this worship.

(ii) Tiberius (A.D. 14–37) could not halt Caesar worship. He forbade temples to be built and priests to be appointed for his own worship; and in a letter to Gython, a Laconian city, he definitely refused divine honours for himself. So far from enforcing Caesar worship, he actively discouraged it.

(iii) Caligula (A.D. 37–41), the next Emperor, was an epileptic, a madman and a megalomaniac. He insisted on divine honours. He attempted to enforce Caesar worship even on the Jews, who had always been and who always were to remain exempt from it. He planned to place his own image in the Holy of Holies in the Temple in Jerusalem, a step which would certainly have provoked unyielding rebellion. Mercifully he died before he could carry out his plans. But in his reign we have an episode when Caesar worship became an imperial demand.

(iv) Caligula was succeeded by Claudius (A.D. 41–54) who completely reversed his insane policy. He wrote to the governor of Egypt—there were a million Jews in Alexandria—fully approving the Jewish refusal to call the Emperor a god and granting them full liberty to enjoy their own worship. On his accession to the throne, he wrote to Alexandria saying: "I deprecate the appointment of a High Priest to me and the erection of temples, for I do not wish to be offensive to my contemporaries, and I hold that sacred fanes and the like have been by all ages attributed to the immortal gods as peculiar honours."

(v) Nero (A.D. 54–68) did not take his own divinity seriously and did nothing to insist on Caesar worship. It is true that he persecuted the Christians; but this was not because they would not worship him, but because he had to find scapegoats for the great fire of Rome.

(vi) On the death of Nero there were three Emperors in eighteen months—Galba, Otto and Vitellius, and in such a time of chaos the question of Caesar worship did not arise.

(vii) The next two Emperors, Vespasian (A.D. 69–79) and Titus (A.D. 79–81), were wise rulers, who made no insistence on Caesar worship.

(viii) The coming of Domitian (A.D. 81–96) brought a complete change. He was a devil. He was the worst of all things— a cold-blooded persecutor. With the exception of Caligula, he was the first Emperor to take his divinity seriously and to *demand* Caesar worship. The difference was that Caligula was an insane devil; Domitian was a sane devil, which is much more terrifying. He erected a monument to "the deified Titus son of the deified Vespasian." He began a campaign of bitter persecution against all who would not worship the ancient gods—"the atheists" as he called them. In particular he launched his hatred against the Jews and the Christians. When he arrived in the theatre with his empress, the crowd were urged to rise and shout: "All hail to our Lord and his Lady!" He enacted that he himself was a god. He informed all provincial governors that government announcements and proclamations must begin: "Our Lord and God Domitian commands . . ." Everyone who addressed him in speech or in writing must begin: "Lord and God."

Here is the background of the *Revelation*. All over the Empire men and women must call Domitian god—or die. Caesar worship was the deliberate policy; all must say: "Caesar is Lord." There was no escape.

What were the Christians to do? What hope had they? They had not many wise and not many mighty. They had no influence or prestige. Against them had risen the might of Rome which no nation had ever resisted. They were confronted with the choice—Caesar or Christ. It was to encourage men in such times that the *Revelation* was written. John did not shut his eyes to the terrors; he saw dreadful things and he saw still more dreadful things on the way; but beyond them he saw glory for those who defied Caesar for the love of Christ. The *Revelation* comes from one of the most heroic ages in all the history of the Christian Church. It is true that Domitian's successor Nerva (A.D. 96–98) repealed the savage laws; but the damage was done, the Christians were outlaws, and the *Revelation* is a clarion call to be faithful unto death in order to win the crown of life.

THE BOOK WORTH STUDYING

No one can shut his eyes to the difficulty of the *Revelation*. It is the most difficult book in the Bible; but it is infinitely worth studying, for it contains the blazing faith of the Christian Church in the days when life was an agony and men expected the end of the heavens and the earth as they knew them but still believed that beyond the terror was the glory and above the raging of men was the power of God.

REVELATION

GOD'S REVELATION TO MEN

Revelation 1: 1–3

> This is the revelation revealed by Jesus Christ, the revelation
> which God gave to him to show to his servants, the revelation
> which tells of the things which must soon happen. This revelation
> Jesus Christ sent and explained through his angel to his servant
> John, who testified to the word sent to him by God and attested
> by the witness borne by Jesus Christ everything which he saw.

THIS book is called sometimes the *Revelation* and sometimes
the *Apocalypse*. It begins with the words "The revelation of
Jesus Christ," which mean not the revelation *about* Jesus
Christ but the revelation given *by* Jesus Christ. The Greek
word for *revelation* is *apokalupsis* which is a word with a
history.

(i) *Apokalupsis* is composed of two parts. *Apo* means *away
from* and *kalupsis* a *veiling*. *Apokalupsis,* therefore, means an
unveiling, a revealing. It was not originally a specially religious
word; it meant simply the disclosure of any fact. There is an
interesting use of it in Plutarch (*How to tell a Flatterer from
a Friend,* 32). Plutarch tells how once Pythagoras severely
rebuked a devoted disciple of his in public and the young man
went out and hanged himself. "From that time on Pythagoras
never admonished anyone when anyone else was present. For
error should be treated as a foul disease, and all admonition
and *disclosure (apokalupsis)* should be in secret." But *apokalupsis* became specially a Christian word.

(ii) It is used for the revealing of God's will to us for our
actions. Paul says that he went up to Jerusalem by *apokalupsis*.
He went because God told him he wanted him to go (*Galatians*
2: 2).

(iii) It is used of the revelation of God's truth to men.

Paul received his gospel, not from men, but by *apokalupsis* from Jesus Christ (*Galatians* 1: 12). In the Christian assembly the message of the preacher is an *apokalupsis* (1 *Corinthians* 14: 6).

(iv) It is used of God's revealing to men of his own mysteries, especially in the incarnation of Jesus Christ (*Romans* 16: 25; *Ephesians* 3: 3).

(v) It is specially used of the revelation of the power and the holiness of God which is to come at the last days. That will be an unveiling of judgment (*Romans* 2: 5); but for the Christian it will be an unveiling of praise and glory (1 *Peter* 1: 7); of grace (1 *Peter* 1: 13); of joy (1 *Peter* 4: 13).

Before we remind ourselves of the more technical use of *apokalupsis*, we may note two things.

(i) This revelation is connected specially with the work of the Holy Spirit (*Ephesians* 1: 17).

(ii) We are bound to see that here we have a picture of the whole of the Christian life. There is no part of it which is not lit by the revelation of God. God reveals to us what we must do and say; in Jesus Christ he reveals himself to us, for he who has seen Jesus has seen the Father (*John* 14: 9); and life moves on to the great and final revelation in which there is judgment for those who have not submitted to God but grace and glory and joy for those who are in Jesus Christ. Revelation is no technical theological idea; it is what God is offering to all who will listen.

Now we look at the technical meaning of *apokalupsis*, for that meaning is specially connected with this book.

The Jews had long since ceased to hope that they would be vindicated as the chosen people by human means. They hoped now for nothing less than the direct intervention of God. To that end they divided all time into two ages—*this present age*, wholly given over to evil; and *the age to come*, the age of God. Between the two there was to be a time of terrible trial. Between the Old and the New Testaments the Jews wrote many books which were visions of the dreadful time before the end and of the blessedness to come. These

books were called *Apokalypses*; and that is what *the Revelation*
is. Although there is nothing like it in the New Testament,
it belongs to a class of literature which was common between
the Testaments. All these books are wild and unintelligible,
for they are trying to describe the indescribable. The very
subject with which *the Revelation* deals is the reason why it
is so difficult to understand.

THE MEANS OF GOD'S REVELATION

Revelation 1: 1-3 (*continued*)

THIS short section gives us a concise account of how revelation comes to men.

(i) Revelation begins with God, the fountain of all truth.
Every truth which men discover is two things—a discovery
of the human mind and a gift of God. But it must always
be remembered that men never *create* the truth; they *receive*
it from God. We must also remember that that reception
comes in two ways. It comes from *earnest seeking*. God gave
men minds and it is often through our minds that he speaks
to us. Certainly he does not grant his truth to the man who
is too lazy to think. It comes from *reverent waiting*. God sends
his truth to the man who not only thinks strenuously, but
waits quietly in prayer and in devotion. But it must be
remembered that prayer and devotion are not simply passive
things. They are the dedicated listening for the voice of God.

(ii) God gives this revelation to Jesus Christ. The Bible
never, as it were, makes a second God of Jesus; rather it
stresses his utter dependence on God. "My teaching," said
Jesus, "is not mine, but his who sent me" (*John* 7: 16).
"I do nothing on my own authority but speak thus as the
Father taught me" (*John* 8: 28). "I have not spoken on my
own authority; the Father who sent me has himself given me
commandment what to say and what to speak" (*John* 12: 49).
It is God's truth that Jesus brings to men; and that is precisely
why his teaching is unique and final.

(iii) Jesus sends that truth to John through his angel (*Revelation* 1:1). Here the writer of the *Revelation* was a child of his day. At this time in history men were specially conscious of the transcendence of God. That is to say, they were impressed above all things with the difference between God and man. So much so that they felt direct communication between God and man was impossible and that there must always be some intermediary. In the Old Testament story Moses received the Law directly from the hands of God (*Exodus* 19 and 20); but twice in the New Testament it is said that the Law was given by angels (*Acts* 7:53; *Galatians* 3:19).

(iv) Finally, the revelation is given to John. It is most uplifting to remember the part men play in the coming of God's revelation. God must find a man to whom he can entrust his truth and whom he can use as his mouthpiece.

(v) Let us note the *content* of the revelation which comes to John. It is the revelation of "the things which *must quickly* happen" (1:1). There are two important words here. There is *must*. History is not haphazard; it has purpose. There is *quickly*. Here is the proof that it is quite wrong to use the *Revelation* as a kind of mysterious timetable of what is going to happen thousands of years from now. As John sees it, the things it deals with are working themselves out immediately. The *Revelation* must be interpreted against the background of its own time.

SERVANTS OF GOD

Revelation 1:1–3 (*continued*)

TWICE the word *servant* appears in this passage. God's revelation was sent to his *servants* and it was sent through his *servant* John. In Greek the word is *doulos* and in Hebrew *ebedh*. Both are difficult fully to translate. The normal translation of *doulos* is *slave*. The real *servant* of God is, in fact, his *slave*. A servant can leave his service when he likes; he has stated hours of work and stated hours of freedom; he works for a wage; he has a mind of his own and can bargain as to when and for what he will give his labour. A slave can do none of these things; he is the absolute possession of his owner, with neither time nor will of his own. *Doulos* and *ebedh* bring out how absolutely we must surrender life to God.

It is of the greatest interest to note to whom these words are applied in Scripture.

Abraham is the servant of God (*Genesis* 26: 24; *Psalm* 105: 26; *Daniel* 9: 11). Jacob is the servant of God (*Isaiah* 44: 1, 2; 45: 4; *Ezekiel* 37: 25). Caleb and Joshua are the servants of God (*Numbers* 14: 24; *Joshua* 24: 29; *Judges* 6: 49; 2 *Chronicles* 24: 6; *Nehemiah* 1: 7; 10: 29; *Psalm* 105: 26; *Daniel* 9: 11). Jacob is the servant of God (*Isaiah* 44: 1, 2; 45: 4; *Ezekiel* 37: 25). Caleb and Joshua are the servants of God (*Numbers* 14: 24; *Joshua* 24: 29; *Judges* 2: 8). David is second only to Moses as characteristically the servant of God (*Psalm* 132: 10; 144: 10; 1 *Kings* 8: 66; 11: 36; 2 *Kings* 19: 34; 20: 6; 1 *Chronicles* 17: 4; in the titles of *Psalms* 18 and 36; *Psalm* 89: 3; *Ezekiel* 34: 24). Elijah is the servant of God (2 *Kings* 9: 36; 10: 10). Isaiah is the servant of God (*Isaiah* 20: 3). Job is the servant of God (*Job* 1: 8; 42: 7). The prophets are the servants of God (2 *Kings* 21: 10; *Amos* 3: 7). The apostles are the servants of God (*Philippians* 1: 1; *Titus* 1: 1; *James* 1: 1; *Jude* 1; *Romans* 1: 1; 2 *Corinthians* 4: 5). A man like Epaphras is the servant of God (*Colossians* 4: 12). All Christians are the servants of God (*Ephesians* 6: 6).

Two things emerge from this.

(i) The greatest men regarded as their greatest honour the fact that they were servants of God.

(ii) We must note the width of this service. Moses, the law-giver; Abraham, the adventurous pilgrim; David, shepherd boy, sweet singer of Israel, king of the nation; Caleb and Joshua, soldiers and men of action; Elijah and Isaiah, prophets and men of God; Job, faithful in misfortune; the apostles, who bore to men the story of Jesus; every Christian—all are *servants of God*. There is none whom God cannot use, if he will submit to his service.

THE BLESSEDS OF GOD

Revelation 1: 1–3 (*continued*)

THIS passage ends with a threefold blessing.

(i) The man who reads these words is blessed. The *reader* here mentioned is not the private reader, but the man who publicly reads the word in the presence of the congregation. The reading of Scripture was the centre of any Jewish service (*Luke* 4: 16; *Acts* 13: 15). In the Jewish synagogue scripture was read to the congregation by seven ordinary members of the congregation, although if a priest or levite was present he took precedence. The Christian Church took much of its service from the synagogue order and the reading of scripture remained a central part of the service. Justin Martyr gives the earliest account of what a Christian service was like; and it includes the reading of "the memoirs of the apostles (i.e. the Gospels), and the writings of the prophets" (Justin Martyr 1: 67). *Reader* became in time an official office in the Church. One of Tertullian's complaints about the heretical sects was the way in which a man could too speedily arrive at office without any training for it. He writes: "And so it comes to pass that today one man is their bishop, and tomorrow another; today he is a deacon who tomorrow is a *reader*" (Tertullian, *On Prescription against Heretics,* 41).

(ii) The man who hears these words is blessed. We do well to remember how great a privilege it is to hear the word of God in our own tongue, a privilege which was dearly bought. Men died to give it to us; and the professional clergy sought for long to keep it to themselves. To this day the task of giving men the Scriptures in their own language goes on.

(iii) The man who keeps these words is blessed. To hear God's word is a privilege; to obey it is a duty. There is no real Christianity in the man who hears and forgets or deliberately disregards.

That is all the more true because the time is short. The time is near (verse 3). The early church lived in vivid expectation of the coming of Jesus Christ and that expectation was "the ground of hope in distress and constant heed to warning." Apart altogether from that, no man knows when the call will come to take him from this earth, and in order to meet God with confidence he must add the obedience of his life to the listening of his ear.

We may note that there are seven *blesseds* in the *Revelation*.

(i) There is the *blessed* we have just studied. We may call it the blessedness of reading, hearing and obeying the Word of God.

(ii) Blessed are the dead who die in the Lord henceforth (14: 13). We may call it the blessedness in heaven of Christ's friends on earth.

(iii) Blessed is he who is awake, keeping his garments (16: 15). We may call it the blessedness of the watchful pilgrim.

(iv) Blessed are those who are invited to the marriage supper of the Lamb (19: 9). We may call it the blessedness of the invited guests of God.

(v) Blessed is he who shares in the first resurrection (20: 6). We may call it the blessedness of the man whom death cannot touch.

(vi) Blessed is he who keeps the words of the prophecy of this book (22: 7). We may call it the blessedness of the wise reader of God's Word.

(vii) Blessed are those who do his commandments (22: 14). We may call it the blessedness of those who hear and obey.

Such blessedness is open to every Christian.

THE MESSAGE AND ITS DESTINATION

Revelation 1: 4–6

This is John writing to the seven Churches which are in Asia. Grace be to you and peace from him who is and who was and who is to come, and from the seven spirits which are before his throne, and from Jesus Christ, the witness on whom you can rely, the first-born of the dead, and the ruler of the kings of the earth. To him who loves us and who set us free from our sins at the cost of

his own blood, and who made us a kingdom, priests to his God
and Father, to him be glory and dominion for ever. Amen.

THE *Revelation* is a letter, written to the *seven Churches which
are in Asia*. In the New Testament Asia is never the con-
tinent but always the Roman province. Once the kingdom of
Attalus the Third, he had willed it to the Romans at his
death. It included the western sea-coast of Asia Minor, on the
shores of the Mediterranean, with Phrygia, Mysia, Caria and
Lycia in the hinterland; and its capital was the city of
Pergamum.

The seven Churches are named in Verse 11—Ephesus,
Smyrna, Pergamum, Thyatira, Sardis, Philadelphia, Laodicea.
These were by no means the only Churches in Asia. There
were Churches at Colossae (*Colossians* 1: 2); Hierapolis
(*Colossians* 4: 13); Troas (2 *Corinthians* 2: 12; *Acts* 20: 5);
Miletus (*Acts* 20: 17); Magnesia and Tralles, as the letters
of Ignatius, the Bishop of Antioch, show. Why did John single
out only these seven? There can be more than one reason
for his selection.

(i) These Churches might be regarded as the centres of
seven postal districts, being all on a kind of ring road which
circled the interior of the province. Troas was off the beaten
track. But Hierapolis and Colossae were within walking
distance of Laodicea; and Tralles, Magnesia and Miletus were
close to Ephesus. Letters delivered to these seven cities would
easily circulate in the surrounding areas; and since every letter
had to be hand-written, each letter would need to be
sent where it would reach most easily the greatest number of
people.

(ii) Any reading of the *Revelation* will show John's pre-
ference for the number seven. It occurs fifty-four times. There
are seven candle-sticks (1: 12), seven stars (1: 16), seven
lamps (4: 5), seven seals (5: 1), seven horns and seven eyes
(5: 6), seven thunders (10: 3), seven angels, plagues and bowls
(15: 6, 7, 8). The ancient peoples regarded seven as the perfect
number, and it runs all through the *Revelation*.

From this certain of the early commentators drew an interesting conclusion. Seven is the perfect number because it stands for *completeness*. It is, therefore, suggested that, when John wrote to *seven* Churches, he was, in fact, writing to the *whole* Church. The first list of New Testament books, called the Muratorian Canon, says of the *Revelation*: "For John also, though he wrote in the *Revelation* to seven Churches, nevertheless speaks to them all." This is all the more likely when we remember how often John says: "He who has an ear, let him hear what the Spirit says to the Churches" (2: 7, 11, 17, 29; 3: 6, 13, 22).

(iii) Although the reasons we have adduced for the choice of these seven Churches may be valid, it may be still more valid that he chose them because in them he had a special authority. They were in a special sense *his* Churches, and by speaking to them he sent a message first to those who knew and loved him best, and then through them to every Church in every generation.

THE BLESSING AND ITS SOURCE

Revelation 1: 4–6 (*continued*)

He begins by sending them the blessing of God.

He sends them *grace*, and this means all the undeserved gifts of the wondrous love of God. He sends them *peace*, which R. C. Charles finely describes as "the harmony restored between God and man through Christ." But there are two extraordinary things in this greeting.

(i) John sends blessings from him who is and who was and who is to come. That is in itself a common title for God. In *Exodus* 3: 14 the word of God to Moses is "I am who I am." The Jewish Rabbis explained that by saying that God meant: "I was; I still am; and in the future I will be." The Greeks spoke of "Zeus who was, Zeus who is, and Zeus who will be." The Orphic worshippers said: "Zeus is the first and Zeus is the last; Zeus is the head and Zeus is the middle;

and from Zeus all things come." This is what in *Hebrews* so beautifully became: "Jesus Christ is the same yesterday, today and for ever" (*Hebrews* 13: 8).

But to get the full meaning of this we must look at it in the Greek, for John bursts the bonds of grammar to show his reverence for God. We translate the first phrase *from him who is*; but that is not what the Greek says. A Greek noun is in the nominative case when it is the subject of a sentence, but, when it is governed by a preposition it changes its case and *its form*. It is so in English. *He* is the subject of a sentence; *him* is the object. When John says that the blessing comes *from him who is* he should have put *him who is* in the genitive case after the preposition; but quite ungrammatically he leaves it in the nominative. It is as if we said in English *from he who is,* refusing to change *he* into *him*. John has such an immense reverence for God that he refuses to alter the form of his name even when the rules of grammar demand it.

John is not finished with his amazing use of language. The second phrase is *from him who was*. Literally, John says *from the he was*. The point is that *who was* would be in Greek a participle. The odd thing is that the verb *eimi* (*to be*) has no past participle. Instead there is used the participle *genomenos* from the verb *gignomai*, which means not only *to be* but also *to become*. *Becoming* implies change and John utterly refuses to apply any word to God that will imply any change; and so he uses a Greek phrase that is grammatically impossible and that no one ever used before.

In the terrible days in which he was writing John stayed his heart on the changelessness of God and used defiance of grammar to underline his faith.

THE SEVENFOLD SPIRIT

Revelation 1: 4–6 (*continued*)

ANYONE who reads this passage must be astonished at the form of the Trinity which we meet here. We speak of Father,

Son and Holy Spirit. Here we have God the Father and Jesus Christ the Son but instead of the Holy Spirit we have *the seven Spirits who are before his throne*. These seven Spirits are mentioned more than once in the *Revelation* (3: 1; 4: 5; 5: 6). Three main explanations have been offered of them.

(i) The Jews talked of the seven angels of the presence, whom they beautifully called "the seven first white ones" (1 *Enoch* 90: 21). They were what we call the archangels, and "they stand and enter before the glory of the Lord" (*Tobit* 12: 15). Their names are not always the same but they are often called Uriel, Rafael, Raguel, Michael, Gabriel, Saiquael and Jeremiel. They had the care of the elements of the world— fire, air and water—and were the guardian angels of the nations. They were the most illustrious and the most intimate servants of God. Some think that they are the seven Spirits mentioned here. But that cannot be; great as the angels were, they were still created beings.

(ii) The second explanation connects them with the famous passage in *Isaiah* 11: 2; as the Septuagint, the Greek version of the Old Testament, has it: "The spirit of the Lord shall rest upon him, the spirit of wisdom and understanding, the spirit of counsel and might, the spirit of knowledge and piety; by this spirit he shall be filled with the fear of God." This passage is the basis of the great conception of *the sevenfold gifts of the Spirit*.

> Come, Holy Ghost, our souls inspire
> And lighten with celestial fire;
> Thou the anointing Spirit art,
> Who dost thy sevenfold gifts impart.

The Spirit, as Beatus said, is one in name but sevenfold in virtues. If we think of the sevenfold gift of the Spirit, it is not difficult to think of the Spirit as seven Spirits, each giving great gifts to men. So it is suggested that the conception of the sevenfold gifts of the Spirit gave rise to the idea of the seven Spirits before the throne of God.

(iii) The third explanation connects the idea of the seven

Spirits with the fact of the seven Churches. In *Hebrews* 2: 4 we read of God giving "gifts of the Holy Spirit." The word translated *gifts* is *merismos*, and it really means *shares*, as if the idea was that God gives a share of his Spirit to every man. So the idea here would be that the seven Spirits stand for the share of the Spirit which God gave to each of the seven Churches. It would mean that no Christian fellowship is left without the presence and the power and the illumination of the Spirit.

THE TITLES OF JESUS

Revelation 1: 4-6 (*continued*)

IN this passage three great titles are ascribed to Jesus Christ.

(i) He is the witness on whom we can rely. It is a favourite idea of the Fourth Gospel that Jesus is a witness of the truth of God. Jesus said to Nicodemus: "Truly, truly, I say to you, we speak of what we know, and bear witness to what we have seen" (*John* 3: 11). Jesus said to Pilate: "For this I have come into the world, to bear witness to the truth" (*John* 18: 37). A witness is essentially a person who speaks from first-hand knowledge. That is why Jesus is God's witness. He is uniquely the person with first-hand knowledge about God.

(ii) He is the first-born of the dead. The word for *first-born* is *prōtotokos*. It can have two meanings. (*a*) It can mean literally *first-born*. If it is used in this sense, the reference must be to the Resurrection. Through his Resurrection Jesus gained a victory over death, which all who believe in him may share. (*b*) Since the first-born was the son who inherited his father's honour and power, *prōtotokos* comes to mean *one with power and honour, one who occupies the first place,* a prince among men. When Paul speaks of Jesus as the first-born of all creation (*Colossians* 1: 15), he means that to him the first place of honour and glory belongs. If we take the word in this sense—and probably we should—it means that Jesus is Lord of the dead as he is Lord of the living. There is no part of the universe, in this world or in the world to come, and nothing in life or in death of which Jesus Christ is not Lord.

(iii) He is the ruler of kings on earth. There are two things to note here. (*a*) This is a reminiscence of *Psalm* 89:27: "I will make him the first-born, the highest of the kings of the earth." That was always taken by Jewish scholars to be a description of the coming Messiah; and, therefore, to say that Jesus is the ruler of kings on earth is to claim that he is the Messiah. (*b*) Swete very beautifully points out the connection between this title of Jesus and the temptation story. In that story the devil took Jesus up into a high mountain and showed him all the kingdoms of the earth and their glory and said: "All these I will give you, if you will fall down and worship me" (*Matthew* 4: 8, 9; *Luke* 4: 6, 7). It was the devil's claim that the kingdoms of the earth were delivered into his power (*Luke* 4: 6); and it was his suggestion that, if Jesus would strike a bargain with him, he would give him a share in them. The amazing thing is that what the devil promised Jesus— and could never have given him—Jesus won for himself by the suffering of the Cross and the power of the Resurrection. Not compromise with evil, but the unswerving loyalty and the unfailing love which accepted the Cross brought Jesus his universal lordship.

WHAT JESUS DID FOR MEN

Revelation 1: 4–6 (*continued*)

FEW passages set down with such splendour what Jesus did for men.

(i) He loves us and he set us free from our sins at the cost of his own blood. The Authorized Version is in error here. It reads: "Unto him that loved us and *washed* us from our sins in his own blood." The words *to wash* and *to set free* are in Greek very alike. *To wash* is *louein*; *to set free* is *luein*; and they are pronounced exactly in the same way. But there is no doubt that the oldest and best Greek manuscripts read *luein*. Again *in his own blood* is a mistranslation. The word translated *in* is *en* which, indeed, can mean *in*; but here it is a translation of the Hebrew word *be* (the *e* is pronounced very short as in *the*), which means *at the price of*.

What Jesus did, as John sees it, is that he freed us from our sins at the cost of his own blood. This is exactly what he says later on when he speaks of those who were ransomed for God by the blood of the Lamb (5: 9). It is exactly what Paul meant when he spoke of us being *redeemed* from the curse of the Law (*Galatians* 3: 13); and when he spoke of *redeeming* those who were under the Law (*Galatians* 4: 5). In both cases the word used is *exagorazein,* which means *to buy out from,* to pay the price of buying a person or a thing out of the possession of him who holds that person or thing in his power.

This is a very interesting and important correction of the Authorized Version. It is made in all the newer translations and it means that the well-worn phrases which speak of being "washed in the blood of the Lamb" have little scriptural authority. These phrases convey a staggering picture; and it must come to many with a certain relief to know that what John said was that we are set free from our sins at the cost of the blood, that is, at the cost of the life of Jesus Christ.

There is another very significant thing here. We must carefully note the tenses of the verbs. John says that Jesus *loves* us and *set us free*. *Loves* is the *present tense* and it means that the love of God in Christ Jesus is something which is continuous. *Set us free* is the *past tense*, the Greek aorist, which tells of one act completed in the past and it means that in the one act of the Cross our liberation from sin was achieved. That is to say, what happened on the Cross was one availing act in time which was an expression of the continuous love of God.

(ii) Jesus made us a kingdom, priests to God. That is a quotation of *Exodus* 19: 6: "You shall be to me a kingdom of priests, and a holy nation." Jesus has done two things for us.

(*a*) He has given us royalty. Through him we may become the true sons of God; and, if we are sons of the King of kings, we are of lineage than which there can be none more royal.

(*b*) He made us priests. The point is this. Under the old way, only the priest had the right of access to God. When a Jew entered the Temple, he could pass through the Court of the Gentiles, the Court of the Women, the Court of the Israelites—but there he must stop; into the Court of the Priests he could not go; no nearer the Holy of Holies could he come. In the vision of the great days to come Isaiah said: "You shall be called the priests of the Lord" (*Isaiah* 61: 6). In that day every one of the people would be a priest and have access to God. That is what John means; because of what Jesus Christ did access to the presence of God is now open to every man. There is a priesthood of all believers. We can come boldly to the throne of grace (*Hebrews* 4: 16), because for us there is a new and living way into the presence of God (*Hebrews* 10: 19–22).

THE COMING GLORY

Revelation 1: 7

> Behold, he is coming with the clouds, and every eye shall see him, and the people who pierced him will see him; and all the tribes of the earth shall lament over him. Yea! Amen!

FROM now on in almost every passage, we shall have to note John's continuous use of the Old Testament. He was so soaked in the Old Testament that it was almost impossible for him to write a paragraph without quoting it. This is interesting and significant. John was living in a time when to be a Christian was an agonizing thing. He himself knew banishment and imprisonment and hard labour; and there were many who knew death in its most cruel forms. The best way to maintain courage and hope in such a situation was to remember that God had never failed in the past; and that his power was not grown less now.

In this passage John sets down the motto and the text of his whole book, his confidence in the triumphant return of Christ, which would rescue Christians in distress from the cruelty of their enemies.

(i) To Christians the return of Christ is a *promise on which to feed the soul*. John takes as his picture of that return *Daniel's* vision of the four bestial powers who have held the world in their grip (*Daniel* 7: 1–14). There was Babylon, the power that was like a lion with eagle's wings (7: 4). There was Persia, the power that was like a savage bear (7: 5). There was Greece, the power that was like a winged leopard (7: 6). There was Rome, a beast with iron teeth, beyond description (7: 7). But the day of these bestial empires was over, and the dominion was to be given to a gentle power like a son of man. "I saw in the night visions, and, behold, with the clouds of heaven there came one like a son of man, and he came to the Ancient of Days, and was presented before him, and to him was given dominion, and glory, and kingdom, that all peoples, nations and languages should serve him" (7: 13, 14). It is from that passage in *Daniel* there emerges the ever-recurring picture of the Son of Man coming on the clouds (*Mark* 13: 26; 14: 62; *Matthew* 24: 30; 26: 64). When we strip away the purely temporary imagery—we, for instance, no longer think of heaven as a localized place above the sky—we are left with the unchanging truth that the day will come when Jesus Christ will be Lord of all. In that hope have ever been the strength and the comfort of Christians for whom life was difficult and for whom faith meant death.

(ii) To the enemies of Christ, *the return of Christ is a threat*. To make this point John again quotes the Old Testament, from *Zechariah* 12: 10 which contains the words: "When they look on him whom they have pierced, they shall mourn for him, as one mourns for an only child, and weep bitterly over him, as one weeps over a first-born." The story behind the *Zechariah* saying is this. God gave his people a good shepherd; but the people in their disobedient folly killed him and took to themselves evil and self-seeking shepherds. But the day will come when in the grace of God they will bitterly repent, and in that day they will look on the good shepherd whom they pierced and will sorrowfully lament for him and for what they have done. John takes that picture and applies it to Jesus. Men crucified him but the day will come when they will look on him again; and this time, he will not be a broken figure on a cross but a regal figure to whom universal dominion has been given.

The first reference of these words is to the Jews and the Romans who actually crucified Jesus. But in every age all who sin crucify him again. The day will come when those who disregarded and those who opposed Jesus Christ will find him the Lord of the universe and the judge of their souls.

The passage closes with the two exclamations—"Even so. Amen!" In the Greek the words are *nai* and *amēn. Nai* is the Greek and *amēn* is the Hebrew for a solemn affirmation— "Yes, indeed! So let it be!" By using the expression both in Greek and Hebrew John underlines its awful solemnity.

THE GOD IN WHOM WE TRUST

Revelation 1 : 8

> I am alpha and omega, says the Lord God, he who is and who was and who is to come, the Almighty.

HERE is a tremendous description of the God in whom we trust and whom we adore.

(i) He is alpha and omega. *Alpha* is the first letter and *omega* the last of the Greek alphabet; and the phrase *alpha to omega* indicates completeness. The first letter of the Hebrew

alphabet is *aleph* and the last is *tau*; and the Jews used the
same kind of expression. The Rabbis said that Adam trans-
gressed the Law and Abraham kept it from *aleph* to *tau*. They
said that God had blessed Israel from *aleph* to *tau*. This
expression indicates that God is absolutely complete: he has
in himself what H. B. Swete called "the boundless life which
embraces all and transcends all."

(ii) God is he who is and who was and who is to come.
That is to say, he is the Eternal. He was before time began;
he is now; and he will be when time ends. He has been the
God of all who have trusted in him; he is the God in whom
at this present moment we can put our trust; and there
can be no event and no time in the future which can separate
us from him.

> Nor death nor life, nor earth nor hell,
>   nor time's destroying sway,
> Can e'er efface us from his heart,
>   or make his love decay.
>
> Each future period that will bless,
>   as it has bless'd the past;
> He lov'd us from the first of time,
>   He loves us to the last.

(iii) God is the Almighty. The word for *Almighty* is
pantokratōr which describes the one who has dominion over
all things.

The suggestive fact is that this word occurs in the New
Testament seven times. Once it occurs in 2 *Corinthians* 6: 18,
in a quotation from the Old Testament, and all the six other
instances are in the *Revelation*. This word is distinctive of
John. Think of the circumstances in which he was writing. The
embattled might of Rome had risen up to crush the Christian
Church. No empire had ever been able to withstand Rome;
what possible chance against Rome had "the panting, huddled
flock whose crime was Christ"? Humanly speaking the Christian Church had none; but if men thought that, they had left

the most important factor of all out of the reckoning—God the *pantokratōr,* in the grip of whose hand were all things.

It is this word which in the Greek Old Testament describes the Lord of Sabaoth, the Lord of hosts (*Amos* 9: 5; *Hosea* 12: 5). It is this word which John uses in the tremendous text: "The Lord our God the Almighty reigns" (*Revelation* 19: 6). If men are in the hands of a God like that, nothing can pluck them away. If behind the Christian Church there is a God like that, so long as she the Church is true to her Lord, nothing can destroy her.

> My times are in thy hand:
>   I'll always trust in thee;
> And, after death, at thy right hand
>   I shall for ever be.

THROUGH TRIBULATION TO THE KINGDOM

Revelation 1: 9

> I, John, your brother and partner in tribulation, in the kingdom, and in that steadfast endurance which life in Christ alone can give, was in the island which is called Patmos, for the sake of the word given by God and confirmed by Jesus Christ.

JOHN introduces himself, not by any official title but as *your brother and partner in tribulation.* His right to speak was that he had come through all that those to whom he was writing were going through. Ezekiel writes in his book: "Then I came to the exiles at Telabib, who dwelt by the river Chebar, and I sat there overwhelmed among them" (*Ezekiel* 3: 15). Men will never listen to one who preaches endurance from the comfort of an easy chair, nor to one who preaches heroic courage to others while he himself has sought a prudent safety. It is the man who has gone through it who can help others who are going through it. As the Indians have it: "No man can criticize another man until he has walked for a day in his moccasins." John and Ezekiel could speak because they had sat where their people were sitting.

John puts three words together—tribulation, kingdom, steadfast endurance. *Tribulation* is *thlipsis*. Originally *thlipsis* meant simply *pressure* and could, for instance, describe the pressure of a great stone on a man's body. At first it was used quite literally, but in the New Testament it has come to describe that pressure of events which is persecution. *Steadfast endurance* is *hupomonē*. *Hupomonē* does not describe the patience which simply passively submits to the tide of events; it describes the spirit of courage and conquest which leads to gallantry and transmutes even suffering into glory. The situation of the Christians was this. They were in *thlipsis* and, as John saw it, in the midst of the terrible events which preceded the end of the world. They were looking towards *basileia,* the kingdom, into which they desired to enter and on which they had set their hearts. There was only one way from *thlipsis* to *basileia*, from affliction to glory, and that was through *hupomonē,* conquering endurance. Jesus said: "He who endures to the end will be saved" (*Matthew* 24: 13). Paul told his people: "Through many tribulations we must enter the kingdom of God" (*Acts* 14: 22). In *Second Timothy* we read: "If we endure, we shall also reign with him" (2 *Timothy* 2: 12).

The way to the kingdom is the way of endurance. But before we leave this passage we must note one thing. That endurance is to be found in Christ. He himself endured to the end and he is able to enable those who walk with him to achieve the same endurance and to reach the same goal.

THE ISLAND OF BANISHMENT

Revelation 1: 9 (*continued*)

JOHN tells us that, when the visions of the *Revelation* came to him, he was in Patmos. It was the unanimous tradition of

the early church that he was banished to Patmos in the reign
of Domitian. Jerome says that John was banished in the
fourteenth year after Nero and liberated on the death of
Domitian (*Concerning Illustrious Men,* 9). This would mean
that he was banished to Patmos about A.D. 94 and liberated
about A.D. 96.

Patmos, a barren rocky little island belonging to a group
of islands called the Sporades, is ten miles long by five miles
wide. It is crescent-shaped, with the horns of the crescent
pointing to the east. Its shape makes it a good natural
harbour. It lies forty miles off the coast of Asia Minor and
it was important because it was the last haven on the voyage
from Rome to Ephesus and the first in the reverse direction.

Banishment to a remote island was a common form of
Roman punishment. It was usually meted out to political
prisoners and, as far as they were concerned, there were
worse punishments. Such banishment involved the loss of civil
rights and all property except enough for a bare existence.
People so banished were not personally ill-treated and were
not confined in prison on their island but free to move within
its narrow limits. Such would be banishment for a political
prisoner; but it would be very different for John. He was a
leader of the Christians and Christians were criminals. The
wonder is that he was not executed straight away. Banishment
for him would involve hard labour in the quarries. Sir
William Ramsay says his banishment would be "preceded by
scourging, marked by perpetual fetters, scanty clothing, insufficient food, sleep on the bare ground, a dark prison, work
under the lash of the military overseer."

Patmos left its mark on John's writing. To this day they
show visitors a cave in a cliff overlooking the sea, where,
they say, the *Revelation* was written. There are magnificent
views of the sea from Patmos, and, as Strahan says, the
Revelation is full of "the sights and the sounds of the
infinite sea." The word *thalassa,* sea, occurs in the *Revelation*
no fewer than twenty-five times. Strahan writes: "Nowhere is
'the voice of many waters' more musical than in Patmos;

nowhere does the rising and setting sun make a more splendid
'sea of glass mingled with fire'; yet nowhere is the longing
more natural that the separating sea should be no more."

It was to all the hardships and pain and weariness of
banishment and hard labour on Patmos that John went *for
the sake of the word given by God.* So far as the Greek goes,
that phrase is capable of three interpretations. It could mean
that John went to Patmos to *preach* the word of God. It
could mean that he withdrew to the loneliness of Patmos to
receive the word of God and the visions of the *Revelation.*
But it is quite certain that it means that it was John's un-
shakeable loyalty to the word of God, and his insistence on
preaching the message of Jesus Christ which brought him to
banishment in Patmos.

IN THE SPIRIT ON THE LORD'S DAY

Revelation 1: 10, 11

> I was in the Spirit on the Lord's Day, and I heard behind me a
> great voice, like the sound of a trumpet, saying: "Write what you
> see in a book, and send it to the seven Churches, to Ephesus and
> to Smyrna, and to Pergamos and to Thyatira and to Sardis and to
> Philadelphia and to Laodicea."

HISTORICALLY this is an extremely interesting passage for it is
the first reference in literature to the Lord's Day.

We have often spoken of the Day of the Lord, that day
of wrath and judgment when this present age with all its
evil was to be shatteringly changed into the age to come. Some
think that John is saying that he was transported in a vision
to that Day of the Lord and saw in advance all the astonishing
things which were to happen then. Those who hold that view
are very few and it is not a natural meaning for the words.

It is quite certain that when John uses the expression
the Lord's Day he is using it as we use it—its very first
mention in literature.

How did the Christian Church cease to observe the Sabbath,

Saturday, and come to observe the Lord's Day, Sunday? The Sabbath commemorated the rest of God after the creation of the world; the Lord's Day commemorates the rising of Jesus from the dead.

The three earliest references to the Lord's Day may well be the following. *The Didachē, The Teaching of the Twelve Apostles,* the first manual of Christian worship and instruction, says of the Christian Church: "On the Lord's Day we meet and break bread" (*Didachē* 14: 1). Ignatius of Antioch, writing to the Magnesians, describes the Christians as "no longer living for the Sabbath, but for the Lord's Day" (Ignatius, *To the Magnesians,* 9: 1). Melito of Sardis wrote a treatise *Concerning the Lord's Day.* By early in the second century the Sabbath had been abandoned and the Lord's Day was the accepted Christian day.

One thing seems certain. All these early references come from Asia Minor and it was there that the observance of the Lord's Day first came in. But what was it that suggested to the Christians a *weekly* observance of the first day of the week? In the east there was a day of the month and a day of the week called *Sebastē,* which means *The Emperor's Day*; it was no doubt this which made the Christians decide that the first day of the week must be dedicated to their Lord.

John was *in the Spirit.* This phrase means that he was in an ecstasy in which he was lifted beyond the things of space and time into the world of eternity. "The Spirit lifted me up," said Ezekiel (*Ezekiel* 3: 12), "and I heard behind me the sound of a great earthquake." For John the voice was like the sound of a trumpet. The sound of the trumpet is woven into the language of the New Testament (*Matthew* 24: 31; 1 *Corinthians* 15: 52; 1 *Thessalonians* 4: 16). There is no doubt that in the mind of John there is here another Old Testament picture. In the account of the giving of the Law it is said: "There were thunders and lightnings, and a thick cloud upon the mountain, and a very loud trumpet blast" (*Exodus* 19: 16). The voice of God sounds with the commanding, unmistakable clarity of a trumpet call.

John is told to write the vision which he sees. It is his duty to share the message which God gives to him. A man must first hear and then transmit, even if the price of the transmission is costly indeed. It may be that a man must withdraw to see his vision, but he must also go forth to tell it.

Two phrases go together. John was *in Patmos*; and John was *in the Spirit*. We have seen what Patmos was like, and we have seen the pain and the hardship that John was undergoing. No matter where a man is, no matter how hard his life, no matter what he is passing through, he may still be in the Spirit. And, if he is in the Spirit, even on Patmos, the glory and the message of God will come to him.

THE DIVINE MESSENGER

Revelation 1: 12, 13

And I turned to see the voice that was speaking to me; and, when I had turned, I saw seven golden lampstands, and, in the midst of the lampstands, one like a son of man, clothed in a robe that reached to his feet, and girt about the breasts with a golden girdle.

WE now begin on the first of John's visions; and we shall see that his mind is so saturated with Scripture that element after element in the picture has an Old Testament background and counterpart.

He says that he turned *to see the voice*. We would say: "I turned to see whose was the voice which was speaking to me."

When he turned, he saw *seven golden lampstands*. John does not only allude to the Old Testament; he takes items from many places in it and out of them he forms a composite picture. The picture of the seven golden lampstands has three sources.

(*a*) It comes from the picture of the candlestick of pure gold in the Tabernacle. It was to have six branches, three on one side and three on the other, and seven lamps to give light (*Exodus* 25: 31–37).

(*b*) It comes from the picture of Solomon's Temple. In it there were to be five candlesticks of pure gold on the right hand and five on the left (1 *Kings* 7: 49).

(*c*) It comes from the vision of Zechariah. Zechariah saw "a candlestick all of gold, with a bowl on the top of it, and seven lamps on it" (*Zechariah* 4: 2).

When John sees a vision, he sees it in terms of scenes from the Old Testament places and occasions when God had already revealed himself to his people. Surely there is a lesson here. The best way to prepare oneself for new revelation of truth is to study the revelation which God has already given.

In the midst of the lampstands he saw one *like a son of man.* Here we are back to the picture of *Daniel* 7: 13, in which the kingdom and the power and the dominion are given by the Ancient of Days to one like a son of man. As we well know from Jesus's use of it, Son of Man became nothing less than the title of the Messiah; and by using it here John makes it plain that the revelation which he is to receive is coming from Jesus Christ himself.

This figure was clothed with *a robe which reached down to his feet,* and he was *girt about the breasts with a golden girdle.* Here again we have three pictures.

(*a*) The word which describes the robe is *podērēs, reaching down to the feet.* This is the word which the Greek Old Testament uses to describe the robe of the High Priest (*Exodus* 28: 4; 29: 5; *Leviticus* 16: 4). Josephus also describes carefully the garments which the priests and the High Priest wore when they were serving in the Temple. They wore "a long robe reaching to the feet," and around the breast, "higher than the elbows," they wore a girdle which was loosely wound round and round the body. The girdle was embroidered with colours and flowers, with a mixture of gold interwoven (Josephus: *The Antiquities of the Jews,* 3.7: 2, 4). All this means that the description of the robe and the girdle of the glorified Christ is almost exactly that of the dress of the priests and of the High Priest. Here, then, is the symbol of the high priestly character of the work of the Risen Lord.

A priest, as the Jews saw it, was a man who himself has access to God and who opens the way for others to come to him; even in the heavenly places Jesus, the great High Priest, is still carrying on his priestly work, opening the way for all men to the presence of God.

(*b*) But other people besides priests wore the long robe reaching to the feet and the high girdle. It was the dress of great ones, of princes and of kings. *Podērēs* is the desccription of the robe of Jonathan (1 *Samuel* 18: 4); of Saul (1 *Samuel* 24: 5, 11); of the princes of the sea (*Ezekiel* 26: 16). The robe the Risen Christ was wearing was the robe of royalty. No longer was he a criminal on a cross; he was dressed like a king.

Christ is Priest and Christ is King.

(*c*) There is still another part of this picture. In the vision of Daniel, the divine figure who came to tell him the truth of God was clothed in fine linen (the Greek Old Testament calls his garment *podērēs*) and girt with fine gold (*Daniel* 10: 5). This, then, is the dress of the messenger of God. So this presents Jesus Christ as the supreme messenger of God.

Here is a tremendous picture. When we trace the origins of the thought of John, we see that by the very dress of the Risen Lord he is showing him to us in his threefold eternal office of Prophet, Priest and King, the one who brings the truth of God, the one who enables others to enter into the presence of God and the one to whom God has given the power and dominion for ever.

THE PICTURE OF THE RISEN CHRIST

Revelation 1: 14–18

His head and his hair were white, as white as wool, like snow; and his eyes were as a flame of fire; and his feet were like beaten brass, as if it had been refined in a furnace; and his voice was as the voice of many waters; he had seven stars in his right hand; and out of his mouth there was coming a sharp two-edged sword;

and his face was as the sun shining in its strength. And when I saw him, I fell at his feet like a dead man. And he put his right hand on me and said: "Stop being afraid. I am the first and the last; I am the living one although I was dead, and, behold, I am alive for ever and ever; and I have the keys of death and of Hades."

BEFORE we begin to look at this passage in detail, there are two general facts we must note.

(i) It is easy to miss seeing how carefully wrought the *Revelation* is. It is not a book which was flung together in a hurry; it is a closely integrated and artistic literary whole. In this passage we have a whole series of descriptions of the Risen Christ; and the interesting thing is that each of the letters to the seven Churches, which follow in the next two chapters, with the exception of the letter to Laodicea, opens with a description of the Risen Christ taken from this chapter. It is as if this chapter sounded a series of themes which were later to become the texts for the letters to the Churches. Let us set down the beginning of each of the first six letters and see how it corresponds to the description of the Risen Christ here.

> To the angel of the Church in Ephesus, write: The words of him *who holds the seven stars in his right hand* (2: 1).

> To the angel of the Church in Smyrna, write: The words of *the first and the last, who died and came to life* (2: 8).

> To the angel of the Church in Pergamum, write: The words of him *who has the sharp two-edged sword* (2: 12).

> To the angel of the Church in Thyatira, write: The words of the Son of God, *who has eyes like a flame of fire, and whose feet are like burnished bronze* (2: 18).

> To the angel of the Church in Sardis, write: The words of him *who has* the seven spirits of God and *the seven stars* (3: 1).

> To the angel of the Church in Philadelphia, write: The words of the holy one, the true one, *who has the key of David,* who opens and no one shall shut, who shuts and no one opens (3: 7).

This is literary craftsmanship of a very high standard.

(ii) The second thing to note is that in this passage John takes titles which in the Old Testament are descriptions of God and applies them to the Risen Christ.

His head and his hair were white, as white wool, like snow.

In *Daniel* 7: 9 that is a description of the Ancient of Days.

His voice was as the sound of many waters.

In *Ezekiel* 43: 2 that is a description of God's own voice.

He had the seven stars in his hand.

In the Old Testament it is God himself who controls the stars. It is God's question to Job: "Can you bind the chains of the Pleiades, or loose the cords of Orion?" (*Job* 38: 31).

I am the first and the last.

Isaiah hears the voice of God saying: "I am the first and I am the last; besides me there is no God" (*Isaiah* 44: 6; cp. 48: 12).

I am the living one.

In the Old Testament God is characteristically "the living God" (*Joshua* 3: 10; *Psalm* 42: 2; *Hosea* 1: 10).

I have the keys of death and of Hades.

The Rabbis had a saying that there were three keys which belonged to God and which he would share with no other —of birth, rain and raising the dead.

Nothing could better show the reverence in which John holds Jesus Christ. He holds him so high that he can give him nothing less than the titles which in the Old Testament belong to God.

> The highest place that heaven affords
>   Is his, is his by right,
> The King of kings, and Lord of lords,
>   And heaven's eternal Light.

THE TITLES OF THE RISEN LORD (1)

Revelation 1: 14–18 *(continued)*

LET us look very briefly at each of the titles by which the Risen Lord is here called.

His head and his hair were white, as white wool, like snow.

This, taken from the description of the Ancient of Days in *Daniel* 7: 9, is symbolic of two things. (*a*) It stands for great age; and it speaks to us of the eternal existence of Jesus Christ. (*b*) It speaks to us of divine purity. The snow and the white wool are the emblems of stainless purity. "Though your sins are like scarlet," said Isaiah, "they shall be as white as snow; though they are red like crimson, they shall become like wool" (*Isaiah* 1: 18). Here we have the symbols of the pre-existence and the sinlessness of Christ.

His eyes were as a flame of fire.

Daniel is always in John's mind, and this is part of the description of the divine figure who brought the vision to Daniel. "His eyes like flaming torches" (*Daniel* 10: 6). When we read the gospel story, we get the impression that he who had once seen the eyes of Jesus could never forget them. Again and again we have the vivid picture of his eyes sweeping round a circle of people (*Mark* 3: 34; 10: 23; 11: 11); sometimes his eyes flashed in anger (*Mark* 3: 5); sometimes they fastened on someone in love (*Mark* 10: 21); and sometimes they had in them all the sorrow of one whose friends had wounded him to the quick (*Luke* 22: 61).

His feet were like beaten brass, as if it had been refined by fire in a furnace.

The word translated *beaten brass* is *chalkolibanos*. No one really knows what the metal is. Perhaps it was that fabulous compound called *electrum*, which the ancients believed to be an alloy of gold and silver and more precious than either. Here again it is the Old Testament which gives John his vision.

In *Daniel* it is said of the divine messenger that "his feet were like the gleam of burnished bronze" (*Daniel* 10: 6); in *Ezekiel* it is said of the angelic beings that "their feet sparkled like burnished bronze" (*Ezekiel* 1: 7). It may be that we are to see two things in the picture. The brass stands for *strength*, for the steadfastness of God; and the shining rays stand for *speed*, for the swiftness of the feet of God to help his own or to punish sin.

His voice was as the sound of many waters.

This is the description of the voice of God in *Ezekiel* 43: 2. But it may be that we can catch an echo of the little island of Patmos. As H. B. Swete has it: "The roar of the Aegean was in the ears of the seer." H. B. Swete goes on to say that the voice of God is not confined to one note. Here it is like the thunder of the sea, but it can also be like a still small voice (1 *Kings* 19: 12), or, as the Greek version of the Old Testament has it, like a gentle breeze. It can thunder a rebuke; and it can croon with the soothing comfort of a mother over her hurt child.

He had seven stars in his right hand.

Here again, we have something which was the prerogative of God alone. But there is also something lovely. When the seer fell in awed terror before the vision of the Risen Christ, the Christ stretched out his right hand and placed it on him and bade him not to be afraid. The hand of Christ is strong enough to uphold the heavens and gentle enough to wipe away our tears.

THE TITLES OF THE RISEN LORD (2)

Revelation 1: 14–18 (*continued*)

There was coming forth from his mouth a sharp, two-edged sword.

THE sword referred to was not long and narrow like a fencer's blade; it was a short, tongue-shaped sword for close fighting. Again the seer has gone here and there in the Old Testament for his picture. Isaiah says of God: "He shall smite the earth with the rod of his mouth" (*Isaiah* 11: 4); and of himself: "He made my mouth like a sharp sword" (*Isaiah* 49: 2). The symbolism tells us of the penetrating quality of the word of God. If we listen to it, no shield of self-deception can withstand it; it strips away our self-deludings, lays bare our sin and leads to pardon. "The word of God is living and active, sharper than any two-edged sword" (*Hebrews* 4: 12). "The Lord will slay the wicked with the breath of his mouth" (2 *Thessalonians* 2: 8).

His face was as the sun shining in its strength.

In *Judges* there is a great picture which may well have been in John's mind. The enemies of God shall perish, "but thy friends be like the sun as he rises in his might" (*Judges* 5: 31). If that is true of them that love God, how much truer it must be of God's beloved Son. Swete sees something even lovelier here, nothing less than a memory of the Transfiguration. On that occasion Jesus was transfigured before Peter, James and John, "and his face shone like the sun" (*Matthew* 17: 2). No one who had seen that sight could ever forget the glow and if the writer of this book is that same John perhaps he saw again on the face of the Risen Christ the glory he had glimpsed on the Mount of Transfiguration.

When I saw him, I fell at his feet like a dead man.

This was the experience of Ezekiel when God spoke to him (*Ezekiel* 1: 28; 3: 23; 43: 3). But surely we can find again a memory of the Gospel story. On that day in Galilee when there was the great catch of fish and Peter glimpsed who Jesus was, he fell down at his knees, conscious only that he was a sinful man (*Luke* 5: 1–11). To the end of the day there can be nothing but reverence in the presence of the holiness and the glory of the Risen Christ.

Stop being afraid.

Surely here, too, we have reminiscence of the Gospel story, for these were words which the disciples had heard more than once from the lips of Jesus. It was thus he spoke to them when he came to them across the water (*Matthew* 14: 27; *Mark* 6: 50); and it was thus above all that he spoke to them on the Mount of Transfiguration, when they were terrified at the sound of the divine voice (*Matthew* 17: 7). Even in heaven, when we come near the unapproachable glory, Jesus is saying: "I am here; do not be afraid."

I am the first and the last.

In the Old Testament this is nothing other than the self-description of God (*Isaiah* 44: 6; 48: 12). It is the promise of Jesus that he is there at the beginning and the end. He is there in the moment of birth and at the time of death. He is there when we set out upon the Christian way and when we finish our course. As F. W. H. Myers makes Paul say:

> Yea thro' life, death, thro' sorrow and thro' sinning
> He shall suffice me, for he hath sufficed:
> Christ is the end, for Christ was the beginning,
> Christ the beginning, for the end is Christ.

I am the living one, although I was dead and I am alive for ever and for ever.

Here is at once the claim and the promise of Christ, the claim of one who conquered death and the promise of one who is alive for evermore to be with his people.

I have the keys of death and Hades.

Death has its gates (*Psalm* 9: 13; 107: 18; *Isaiah* 38: 10); and Christ has the keys of these gates. There were those who took this claim—and some still do—as a reference to the descent into hell (1 *Peter* 3: 18–20). There was a conception in the ancient Church that when Jesus descended into Hades, he unlocked the doors and brought out Abraham and all God's faithful people who had lived and died in the generations before. But we may take it in an even wider sense;

for we who are Christians believe that Jesus Christ has abolished death and brought life and immortality to light through the gospel (2 *Timothy* 1: 10), that because he lives we shall live also (*John* 14: 19), and that, therefore, for us and for those whom we love the bitterness of death is for ever past.

THE CHURCHES AND THEIR ANGELS

Revelation 1: 20

> Here is the secret meaning of the seven stars which you saw in my right hand and the seven golden lampstands. The seven stars are the angels of the seven Churches and the seven lampstands are the seven Churches.

THIS passage begins with a word which throughout the New Testament is used in a very special case. The Authorized Version speaks of the *mystery* of the seven stars and of the seven golden candlesticks. The Greek, *mustērion,* does not mean a *mystery* in our sense of the term. It means something which is meangingless to the outsider but meangingful to the initiate who possesses the key. So here the Risen Christ goes on to give the inner meaning of the seven stars and the seven lampstands.

The seven lampstands stand for the seven Churches. One of the great titles of the Christian is that he is the light of the world (*Matthew* 5: 14; *Philippians* 2: 15). But one of the old Greek commentators has a penetrating comment on this. He says that the Churches are called, not the light itself, but the lampstand on which the light is set. It is not the Churches themselves which produce the light; the giver of light is Jesus Christ; and the Churches are only the vessels within which the light shines. The Christian's light is always a borrowed light.

One of the great problems of the *Revelation* is to decide what John means by the *angels of the Churches.* More than one explanation has been offered.

(i) The word *aggelos—gg* in Greek is pronounced *ng*—
has two meanings. It means an *angel*; but far oftener it means
a *messenger*. It is suggested that messengers of all the Churches
have assembled to receive a message from John and take it
back to their congregations. If that is so, each letter will
begin: "To the messenger of the Church of. . . ." As far as
the Greek goes this is perfectly possible; and it gives good
sense; but the difficulty is that *aggelos* is used in the *Revelation*
about fifty times apart from its use here and in the letters to the
seven Churches, and without exception it means *angel*.

(ii) It is suggested that *aggelos* means a bishop of the
Churches. It is suggested, either that the bishops of the
Churches have gathered to meet John or that he is directing
these letters to them. In favour of this theory there is quoted
the words of Malachi: "The lips of a priest should guard
knowledge, and men should seek instruction from his mouth,
for he is the *messenger* of the Lord of hosts" (*Malachi* 2: 7).
In the Greek Old Testament *messenger* is *aggelos*; and it is
suggested that the title could very easily be transferred to the
bishops of the Churches. They are the messengers of the Lord
to their Churches and to them John speaks. Again this explanation gives good sense; but it suffers from the same objection
as the first. It attaches *aggelos* to a human person and that
John never elsewhere does.

(iii) It is suggested that this has to do with the idea of
guardian angels. In Hebrew thought every nation had its
presiding angel (cp. *Daniel* 10: 13, 20, 21). Michael, for
instance, was held to be the guardian angel of Israel (*Daniel*
12: 1). People, too, had their guardian angels. When Rhoda
came with the news that Peter had escaped from prison,
they would not believe her and said it was his angel (*Acts*
12: 15). Jesus himself spoke of the angels who guard a little
child (*Matthew* 18: 10). If we take it in this sense, the difficulty
is that then the guardian angels of the Churches are
being rebuked for the sins of the Churches. In fact Origen
believed that this was the case. He said that the guardian
angel of a Church was like the tutor of a child. If a child

went wrong, the tutor was blamed; and if a Church went wrong, God in his mercy blamed its angel. The difficulty is that, though the angel of the Church is mentioned in the address of each letter, undoubtedly it is the members of the Church who are being addressed.

(iv) Both Greeks and Jews believed that every earthly thing had a heavenly counterpart; and it is suggested that the angel is the ideal of the Church; and that the Churches are being addressed as their ideal selves to bring them back to the right way.

None of the explanations is fully satisfactory; but maybe the last is the best, for there is no doubt that in the letters the angel and the Church are one and the same.

We now go on to study the letters to the Seven Churches. In each case we shall give an outline of the history and the contemporary background of the city in which the Church was; and once we have studied the general background we will go on to study each letter in detail.

THE LETTER TO EPHESUS

Revelation 2: 1–7

To the angel of the Church in Ephesus, write:

These things says he who holds the seven stars in his right hand and who walks in the midst of the seven golden lampstands.

I know your works—I mean your toil and your steadfast endurance, and I know that you cannot bear evil men, and that you have put to the test those who call themselves apostles, and who are not, and have proved them liars. I know that you possess steadfast endurance. I know all that you have borne for my name's sake and I know that you have not been worn out by your efforts. All the same I have this against you—that you have left your first love. Remember, then, whence you have fallen, and repent, and make your conduct such as it was at first. If you do not, I am coming to you, and I will remove your lampstand from its place, if you do not repent.

But you do possess this virtue—you hate the works of the Nicolaitans, which I too hate.

Let him who has an ear hear what the Spirit is saying to the Churches. I will give to him who overcomes to eat of the tree of life, which is in the Paradise of God.

EPHESUS,
FIRST AND GREATEST

Revelation 2: 1–7

WHEN we know something of the history of Ephesus and learn something of its conditions at this time, it is easy to see why it comes first in the list of the seven Churches.

Pergamum was the official capital of the province of Asia but Ephesus was by far its greatest city. It claimed as its proud title "The first and the greatest metropolis of Asia." A Roman writer called it *Lumen Asiae,* The Light of Asia. Let us see, then, the factors which gave it its pre-eminent greatness.

(i) In the time of John, Ephesus was the greatest harbour in Asia. All the roads of the Cayster Valley—the Cayster was the river on which it stood—converged upon it. But the roads came from further afield than that. It was at Ephesus that the road from the far-off Euphrates and Mesopotamia reached the Mediterranean, having come by way of Colossae and Laodicea. It was at Ephesus that the road from Galatia reached the sea, having come by way of Sardis. And from the south came up the road from the rich Maeander Valley. Strabo, the ancient geographer, called Ephesus "The Market of Asia," and it may well be that in *Revelation* 18: 12, 13 John was setting down a description of the varied riches of the market-place at Ephesus.

Ephesus was the Gateway of Asia. One of its distinctions, laid down by statute, was that when the Roman proconsul came to take up office as governor of Asia, he must disembark at Ephesus and enter his province there. For all the travellers and the trade, from the Cayster and the Maeander Valleys, from Galatia, from the Euphrates and from Mesopotamia, Ephesus was the highway to Rome. In later times, when the Christians were brought from Asia to be flung to the lions in the arena in Rome, Ignatius called Ephesus the Highway of the Martyrs.

Its position made Ephesus the wealthiest and the greatest

city in all Asia and it has been aptly called the Vanity Fair
of the ancient world.

(ii) Ephesus had certain important political distinctions. It
was a *free city*. In the Roman Empire certain cities were free
cities; they had had that honour conferred upon them because
of their services to the Empire. A free city was within its
own limits self-governing; and it was exempted from ever
having Roman troops garrisoned there. It was an *assize town*.
The Roman governors made periodical tours of their provinces; and at certain specially chosen cities and towns courts
were held where the governor tried the most important cases.
Further, Ephesus held yearly the most famous games in Asia
which attracted people from all over the province.

(iii) Ephesus was the centre of the worship of Artemis or,
as the Authorized Version calls her, Diana of the Ephesians.
The Temple of Artemis was one of the seven wonders of the
ancient world. It was four hundred and twenty-five feet long
by two hundred and twenty feet wide; it had one hundred
and twenty columns, each sixty feet high and the gift of a
king, and thirty-six of them were richly gilded and inlaid.
Ancient temples consisted mostly of colonnades with only
the centre portion roofed over. The centre portion of the
Temple of Artemis was roofed over with cypress wood.
The image of Artemis was one of the most sacred images in the
ancient world. It was by no means beautiful but a squat, black,
many-breasted figure; so ancient that none knew its origin. We
have only to read *Acts* 19 to see how precious Artemis and
her temple were to Ephesus. Ephesus had also famous temples
to the godhead of the Roman Emperors, Claudius and Nero,
and in after days was to add temples to Hadrian and
Severus. In Ephesus pagan religion was at its strongest.

(iv) Ephesus was a notorious centre of pagan superstition.
It was famous for the *Ephesian Letters,* amulets and charms
which were supposed to be infallible remedies for sickness,
to bring children to those who were childless and to ensure
success in any undertaking; and people came from all over the
world to buy them.

(v) The population of Ephesus was very mixed. Its citizens were divided into six tribes. One consisted of those who were descendants of the original natives of the country; one consisted of those who were direct descendants of the original colonists from Athens; three consisted of other Greeks; and one, it is probable, consisted of Jews. Besides being a centre of religion the Temple of Artemis was also a centre of crime and immorality. The Temple area possessed the right of asylum; any criminal was safe if he could reach it. The temple possessed hundreds of priestesses who were sacred prostitutes. All this combined to make Ephesus a notoriously evil place. Heraclitus, one of the most famous of ancient philosophers, was known as "the weeping philosopher." His explanation of his tears was that no one could live in Ephesus without weeping at its immorality.

Such was Ephesus; a more unpromising soil for the sowing of the seed of Christianity can scarcely be imagined; and yet it was there that Christianity had some of its greatest triumphs. R. C. Trench writes: "Nowhere did the word of God find a kindlier soil, strike root more deeply or bear fairer fruits of faith and love."

Paul stayed longer in Ephesus than in any other city (*Acts* 20: 31). It was with Ephesus that Timothy was connected so that he is called its first bishop (1 *Timothy* 1: 3). It is in Ephesus that we find Aquila, Priscilla and Apollos (*Acts* 18: 19, 24, 26). Surely to no one was Paul ever more close than to the Ephesian elders, as his farewell address so beautifully shows (*Acts* 20: 17–38). In later days John was the leading figure of Ephesus. Legend has it that he brought Mary the mother of Jesus to Ephesus and that she was buried there. When Ignatius of Antioch wrote to Ephesus, on his way to being martyred in Rome, he could write: "You were ever of one mind with the apostles in the power of Jesus Christ."

There can be few places which better prove the conquering power of the Christian faith.

We may note one more thing. We have spoken of Ephesus as the greatest harbour of Asia. Today there is little left of

Ephesus but ruins and it is no less than six miles from the sea. The coast is now "a harbourless line of sandy beach, unapproachable by a ship." What was once the Gulf of Ephesus and the harbour is "a marsh dense with reeds." It was ever a fight to keep the harbour of Ephesus open because of the silt which the Cayster brings down. The fight was lost and Ephesus vanished from the scene.

EPHESUS
CHRIST AND HIS CHURCH

Revelation 2: 1–7 (*continued*)

JOHN begins the letter to Ephesus with two descriptions of the Risen Christ.

(i) He holds the seven stars in his right hand. That is to say, Christ holds the Churches in his hand. The word for to hold is *kratein*, and it is a strong word. It means that Christ has complete control over the Church. If the Church submits to that control, it will never go wrong; and more than that— our security lies in the fact that we are in the hand of Christ. "They shall never perish, and no one shall snatch them out of my hand" (*John* 10: 28).

There is another point here which emerges only in the Greek. *Kratein* normally takes a genitive case after it (the case which in English we express by the word *of*). Because, when we take hold of a thing, we seldom take hold of *the whole of it* but of *part of it*. When *kratein* takes an accusative after it, it means that the whole object is gripped within the hand. Here, *kratein* takes the accusative and that means that Christ clasps the whole of the seven stars in his hand. That means he holds *the whole Church* in his hand.

We do well to remember that. It is not only *our* Church which is in the hand of Christ; the *whole* Church is in his hand. When men put up barriers between Church and Church, they do what Christ never does.

(ii) He walks in the midst of the seven golden lampstands.

The lampstands are the Churches. This expression tells us of
Christ's unwearied activity in the midst of his Churches. He
is not confined to any one of them; wherever men are met to
worship in his name, Christ is there.

John goes on to say certain things about the people of
the Church of Ephesus.

(i) The Risen Christ praises their *toil*. The word is *kopos*
and it is a favourite New Testament word. Tryphena,
Tryphosa and Persis all *work hard* in the Lord (*Romans* 16: 12).
The one thing that Paul claims is that he has *worked harder*
than all (1 *Corinthians* 15: 10). He fears lest the Galatians
slip back, and his *labour* is in vain (*Galatians* 4: 11). In each
case—and there are many others—the word is either *kopos*
or the verb *kopian*. The special characteristic of these words is
that they describe the kind of toil which takes everything of
mind and sinew that a man can put into it. The Christian
way is not for the man who fears to break sweat. The
Christian is to be a toiler for Christ, and, even if physical
toil is impossible, he can still toil in prayer.

(ii) The Risen Christ praises their *steadfast endurance*. Here
is the word *hupomonē* which we have come upon again and
again. It is not the grim patience which resignedly accepts
things. It is the courageous gallantry which accepts suffering
and hardship and turns them into grace and glory. It is often
said that suffering colours life; but when we meet life with
the *hupomonē* which Christ can give, the colour of life is
never grey or black; it is always tinged with glory.

EPHESUS
WHEN ORTHODOXY COSTS TOO MUCH

Revelation 2: 1-7 (*continued*)

THE Risen Christ goes on to praise the Christians of Ephesus
because they have tested evil men and proved them liars.

Many an evil man came into the little congregations of

the early church. Jesus had warned of the false prophets who
are wolves in sheep's clothing (*Matthew* 7: 15). In his farewell speech to the elders of this very Church at Ephesus,
Paul had warned them that grievous wolves would invade the
flock (*Acts* 20: 29). These evil men were of many kinds. There
were emissaries of the Jews who sought to entangle Christians
again in the Law and followed Paul everywhere, trying to
undo his work. There were those who tried to turn liberty
into licence. There were professional beggars who preyed on
the charity of the Christian congregations. The Church at
Ephesus was even more open to these itinerant menaces than
any other Church. It was on the highway to Rome and to the
east, and what R. C. Trench called "the whole rabble of evil-
doers" was liable to descend upon it.

More than once the New Testament insists on the necessity
of testing. John in his First Letter ˈ that the spirits who
claim to come fɪ by their willingness
to accept the Iɪ s (1 *John* 4: 1–3).
Paul insists that ᴜould test all things and
then hold on to that which is good (1 *Thessalonians* 5: 21).
He insists that, when the prophets preach, they are subject
to the testing of the other prophets (1 *Corinthians* 14: 29). A
man cannot proclaim his private views in the assembly of
God's people; he must abide in the tradition of the Church.
Jesus demanded the hardest test of all: "By their fruits you
will know them" (*Matthew* 7: 15–20).

The Church at Ephesus had faithfully applied its tests and
had weeded out all evil and misguided men; but the trouble
was that something had got lost in the process. "I have this
against you," says the Risen Christ, "that you have lost your
first love." That phrase may have two meanings.

(*a*) It can mean that the first enthusiasm is gone. Jeremiah
speaks of the devotion of Israel to God in the early days.
God says to the nation that he remembers, "the devotion of
your youth, your love as a bride" (*Jeremiah* 2: 2). There had
been a honeymoon period, but the first flush of enthusiasm
is past. It may be that the Risen Christ is saying that all the

enthusiasm has gone out of the religion of the Church of Ephesus.

(*b*) Much more likely this means that the first fine rapture of love for the brotherhood is gone. In the first days the members of the Church at Ephesus had really loved each other; dissension had never reared its head; the heart was ready to kindle and the hand was ready to help. But something had gone wrong. It may well be that heresy-hunting had killed love and orthodoxy had been achieved at the price of fellowship. When that happens, orthodoxy has cost too much. All the orthodoxy in the world will never take the place of love.

EPHESUS
THE STEPS ON THE RETURN JOURNEY

Revelation 2: 1–7 (*continued*)

In Ephesus something had gone wrong. The earnest toil was there; the gallant endurance was there; the unimpeachable orthodoxy was there; but the love was gone. So the Risen Christ makes his appeal and it is for the three steps of the return journey.

(i) First, he says *Remember*. He is not here speaking to someone who has never been inside the Church; he is speaking to those who are inside but have somehow lost the way. Memory can often be the first step on the way back. In the far country the prodigal son suddenly remembered his home (*Luke* 15: 17).

O. Henry has a short story. There was a lad who had been brought up in a village; and in the village school he had sat beside a village girl, innocent and sweet. The lad found his way to the city; fell into bad company; became an expert pickpocket. He was on the street one day; he had just picked a pocket—a neat job, well done—and he was pleased with himself. Suddenly he saw the girl he used to sit beside at school. She was still the same—innocent and sweet. She did not see him; he took care of that. But suddenly he remembered what

he had been, and realized what he was. He leaned his burning head against the cool iron of a lamp post. "God," he
said, "how I hate myself." Memory was offering him the way
back.

William Cowper wrote:

> Where is the blessedness I knew
> When first I saw the Lord?
> Where is the soul-refreshing view
> Of Jesus and his word?

A verse like that may sound like nothing but tragedy and
sorrow, but in fact it can be the first step of the way back;
for the first step to amendment is to realize that something
has gone wrong.

(ii) Second, he says *Repent*. When we discover that something has gone wrong, there is more than one possible reaction.
We may feel that nothing can sustain its first lustre, and so
accept what we consider inevitable. We may be filled with
a feeling of resentment and blame life instead of facing ourselves. We may decide that the old thrill is to be found along
forbidden pathways and try to find spice for life in sin. But the
Risen Christ says, "Repent!" Repentance is the admission that
the fault is ours and the feeling of sorrow for it. The prodigal's
reaction is: "I will arise and go to my father and say I have
sinned." (*Luke* 15: 18). It is Saul's cry of the heart when he
realizes his folly: "I have played the fool and I have erred
exceedingly" (1 *Samuel* 26: 21). The hardest thing about
repentance is the acceptance of personal responsibility for our
failure, for once the responsibility is accepted the godly sorrow
will surely follow.

(iii) Third, he says *Do*. The sorrow of repentance is meant
to drive a man to two things. First, it is meant to drive
him to fling himself on the grace of God, saying only: "God,
be merciful to me a sinner." Second, it is meant to drive
him to action in order to bring forth fruits meet for repentance. No man has truly repented when he does the same
things again. Fosdick said that the great truth of Christianity

is that "no man need stay the way he is." The proof of repentance is a changed life, a life changed by our effort in co-operation with the grace of God.

EPHESUS
A RUINOUS HERESY

Revelation 2: 1-7 (*continued*)

WE meet here a heresy which the Risen Christ says that he hates and which he praises Ephesus for also hating. It may seem strange to attribute hatred to the Risen Christ; but two things are to be remembered. First, if we love anyone with passionate intensity, we will necessarily hate anything which threatens to ruin that person. Second, it is necessary to hate the sin but love the sinner.

The heretics we meet here are the Nicolaitans. They are only named, not defined. But we meet them again in Pergamum (verse 15). There they are very closely connected with those "who hold the teaching of Balaam," and that in turn is connected with eating things offered to idols and with immorality (verse 14). We meet precisely the same problem at Thyatira where the wicked Jezebel is said to cause Christians to practise immorality and to eat things offered to idols.

We may first note that this danger is coming not from outside the Church but from inside. The claim of these heretics was that they were not destroying Christianity but presenting an improved version.

We may, second, note that the Nicolaitans and those who hold the teaching of Balaam were, in fact, one and the same. There is a play on words here. The name *Nicolaus*, the founder of the Nicolaitans, could be derived from two Greek words, *nikan, to conquer,* and *laos, the people. Balaam* can be derived from two Hebrew words, *bela,* to *conquer,* and *ha'am, the people*. The two names, then, are the same and both can describe an evil teacher, who has won victory over the people and subjugated them to poisonous heresy.

In *Numbers* 25: 1-5 we find a strange story in which the

Israelites were seduced into illegal and sacrilegious unions with Moabite women and into the worship of Baal-peor, a seduction which, if it had not been sternly checked, might have ruined the religion of Israel and destroyed her as a nation. When we go on to *Numbers* 31: 16 we find that seduction definitely attributed to the evil influence of Balaam. Balaam, then, in Hebrew history stood for an evil man who seduced the people into sin.

Let us now see what the early church historians have to tell us about these Nicolaitans. The majority identify them with the followers of Nicolaus, the proselyte of Antioch, who was one of the seven commonly called deacons (*Acts* 6: 5). The idea is that Nicolaus went wrong and became a heretic. Irenaeus says of the Nicolaitans that "they lived lives of unrestrained indulgence" (*Against Heresies,* 1.26.3). Hippolytus says that he was one of the seven and that "he departed from correct doctrine, and was in the habit of inculcating indifference of food and life" (*Refutation of Heresies,* 7: 24). *The Apostolic Constitutions* (6: 8) describe the Nicolaitans as "shameless in uncleanness." Clement of Alexandria says they "abandon themselves to pleasure like goats . . . leading a life of self-indulgence." But he acquits Nicolaus of all blame and says that they perverted his saying "that the flesh must be abused." Nicolaus meant that the body must be kept under; the heretics perverted it into meaning that the flesh can be used as shamelessly as a man wishes (*The Miscellanies* 2: 20). The Nicolaitans obviously taught loose living.

Let us see if we can identify their point of view and their teaching a little more definitely. The letter to Pergamum tells us that they seduced people into eating meat offered to idols and into immorality. When we turn to the decree of the Council of Jerusalem, we find that two of the conditions on which the Gentiles were to be admitted to the Church were that they were to abstain from things offered to idols and from immorality (*Acts* 15: 28, 29). These are the very conditions that the Nicolaitans broke.

They were almost certainly people who argued on these

lines. (*a*) The Law is ended; therefore, there are no laws and we are entitled to do what we like. They confused Christian liberty with unchristian licence. They were the very kind of people whom Paul urged not to use their liberty as an opportunity for the flesh (*Galatians* 5: 13). (*b*) They probably argued that the body is evil anyway and that a man could do what he liked with it because it did not matter. (*c*) They probably argued that the Christian was so defended by grace that he could do anything and take no harm.

What lay behind this Nicolaitan perversion of the truth? The trouble was the necessary difference between the Christian and the pagan society in which he moved. The heathen had no hesitation in eating meat offered to idols and it was set before him at every social occasion. Could a Christian attend such a feast? The heathen had no idea of chastity and sexual relations outside marriage were accepted as completely normal and brought no shame. Must a Christian be so very different? The Nicolaitans were suggesting that there was no reason why a Christian should not come to terms with the world. Sir William Ramsay describes their teaching thus: "It was an attempt to effect a reasonable compromise with the established usages of the Graeco-Roman society and to retain as many as possible of those usages in the Christian system of life." This teaching naturally affected most the upper classes because they had most to lose if they went all the way with the Christian demand. To John the Nicolaitans were worse than pagans, for they were the enemy within the gates.

The Nicolaitans were not prepared to be different; they were the most dangerous of all heretics from a practical point of view, for, if their teaching had been successful, the world would have changed Christianity and not Christianity the world.

EPHESUS
THE GREAT REWARD

Revelation 2: 1-7 (*continued*)

FINALLY, the Risen Christ makes his great promise to those

who overcome. In this picture there are two very beautiful conceptions.

(i) There is the conception of *the tree of life.* This is part of the story of the Garden of Eden; in the midst of the garden there was the tree of life (*Genesis* 2: 9); it was the tree of which Adam was forbidden to eat (*Genesis* 2: 16, 17); the tree whose fruit would make a man like God, and for eating which Adam and Eve were driven from Eden (*Genesis* 3: 22–24).

In later Jewish thought the tree came to stand for that which gave man life indeed. Wisdom is a tree of life to them that lay hold of her (*Proverbs* 3: 18); the fruit of the righteous is a tree of life (*Proverbs* 11: 30); hope fulfilled is a tree of life (*Proverbs* 13: 12); a tongue is a tree of life (*Proverbs* 15: 4).

To this is to be added another picture. Adam was first forbidden to eat of the tree of life and then he was barred from the garden so that the tree of life was lost for ever. But it was a regular Jewish conception that, when the Messiah came and the new age dawned, the tree of life would be in the midst of men and those who had been faithful would eat of it. The wise man side: "They that do the things that please thee shall receive the fruit of the tree of immortality" (*Ecclesiasticus* 19: 19). The rabbis had a picture of the tree of life in paradise. Its boughs overshadowed the whole of paradise; it had five hundred thousand fragrant perfumes and its fruit as many pleasant tastes, every one of them different. The idea was that what Adam had lost the Messiah would restore. To eat of the tree of life means to have all the joys that the faithful conquerors will have when Christ reigns supreme.

(ii) There is the conception of *paradise,* and the very sound of the word is lovely. It may be that we do not attach any very definite meaning to it but when we study history, we come upon some of the most adventurous thinking the world has ever known.

(*a*) Originally paradise was a Persian word. Xenophon wrote much about the Persians, and it was he who introduced the word into the Greek language. Originally it meant a pleasure garden. When Xenophon is describing the state in which the Persian king lived, he says that he takes care that, wherever he resides, there are *paradises,* full of all the good and beautiful things the soil can produce (Xenophon: *Oeconomicus,* 4: 13). Paradise is a lovely word to describe a thing of serene beauty.

(*b*) In the Septuagint paradise has two uses. First, it is regularly used for the *Garden* of Eden (*Genesis* 2: 8; 3: 1). Second, it is regularly used of any stately garden. When Isaiah speaks of a *garden* that has no water, it is the word *paradise* that is used (*Isaiah* 1: 30). It is the word used when Jeremiah says: "Plant *gardens* and eat their produce" (*Jeremiah* 29: 5). It is the word used when the preacher says: "I made myself gardens and parks, and planted in them all kinds of fruit trees" (*Ecclesiastes* 2: 5).

(iii) In early Christian thought the word has a special meaning. In Jewish thought after death the souls of all alike went to Hades, a grey and shadowy place. Early Christian thought conceived of an intermediate state between earth and heaven to which all men went and in which they remained until the final judgment. This place was conceived of by Tertullian as a vast cavern beneath the earth. But there was a special part in which the patriarchs and the prophets lived, and that was paradise. Philo describes it as a place "vexed by neither rain, nor snow, nor waves, but which the gentle Zephyr refreshes, breathing ever on it from the ocean." As Tertullian saw it, only one kind of person went straight to this paradise, and that was the martyr. "The sole key," he said, "to unlock paradise is your own life's blood" (Tertullian: *Concerning the Soul,* 55).

Origen was one of the most adventurous thinkers the Church ever produced. He writes like this: "I think that all the saints (*saints* means *Christians*) who depart from this life will remain in some place situated on the earth, which holy Scripture calls paradise, as in some place of instruction and, so to speak, class-room or school of souls. . . . If anyone indeed be

pure in heart and holy in mind, and more practised in
perception, he will by making more rapid progress, quickly
ascend to a place in the air, and reach the kingdom of
heaven, through these mansions (*stages*) which the Greeks
called *spheres* and which holy Scripture calls *heavens*. . . . He
will in the end follow him who has passed into the heavens,
Jesus the Son of God, who said: 'I will that where I am,
these may be also.' It is of this diversity of places he speaks,
when he said: 'In my Father's house are many mansions'"
(Origen: *De Principilis*, 2: 6).

The great early thinkers did not identify paradise and
heaven; paradise was the intermediate stage, where the souls
of the righteous were fitted to enter the presence of God. There
is something very lovely here. Who has not felt that the leap
from earth to heaven is too great for one step and that
there is need of a gradual entering into the presence of God?
May it have been of this that Charles Wesley was thinking
when he sang:

> *Changed from glory into glory,*
>   Till in heaven we take our place,
> Till we cast our crowns before thee,
>   Lost in wonder, love, and praise.

(iv) In the end in Christian thought paradise did not retain
this idea of an intermediate state. It came to be equivalent to
heaven. Our minds must turn to the words of Jesus to the
dying and penitent thief: "Today you will be with me in paradise" (*Luke* 23: 43). We are in the presence of mysteries about
which it would be irreverent to dogmatize; but is there any
better definition of paradise than to say that it is life for ever
in the presence of our Lord?

> When death these mortal eyes shall seal,
>   And still this throbbing heart,
> The rending veil shall thee reveal
>   All glorious as thou art—

and that is paradise.

THE LETTER TO SMYRNA

Revelation 2: 8–11

And to the angel of the Church in Smyrna, write:

These things says the first and the last, who passed through death, and who came to life again.

I know the affliction and the poverty you endure—you are rich in spite of it—and I know the slanders which proceed from those who call themselves Jews and are not, but who are a synagogue of Satan. Have no fear of what you will have to go through. Behold! the devil is going to throw some of you into prison in order to test you, and you will have a time of affliction which will last for ten days. Show yourselves loyal to death and I will give you the crown of life.

Let him who has an ear hear what the Spirit is saying to the Churches. He who overcomes will not be hurt by the second death.

SMYRNA
THE CROWN OF ASIA

Revelation 2: 8–11

IF it was inevitable that Ephesus should come first in the list of the seven Churches, it was but natural that Smyrna its great rival should come second. Of all the cities of Asia, Smyrna was the loveliest. Men called it the ornament of Asia, the crown of Asia and the flower of Asia. Lucian said that it was "the fairest of the cities of Ionia." Aristides, who sang the praise of Smyrna with such splendour, spoke of "the grace which extends over every part like a rainbow . . . the brightness which pervades every part, and reaches up to the heavens, like the glitter of the bronze of armour in Homer." It added to the charm of Smyrna that the west wind, the gentle zephyr ever blew through its streets. "The wind," said Aristides, "blows through every part of the city, and makes it as fresh as a grove of trees." The constant west wind had only one disadvantage. The sewage of the city drained into the gulf on which the city stood, and the west wind tended to blow it back upon the city rather than out to sea.

Smyrna was magnificently situated. It stood at the end of the road which crossed Lydia and Phrygia and travelled out to the far east, and it commanded the trade of the rich Hermus valley. Inevitably it was a great trading city. The city itself stood at the end of a long arm of the sea, which ended in a small land-locked harbour in the city's heart. It was the safest of all harbours and the most convenient; and it had the added advantage that in time of war it could be easily closed by a chain across its mouth. It was fitting that on the coins of Smyrna there should be an inscription of a merchant ship ready for sea.

The setting of the city was equally beautiful. It began at the harbour; it traversed the narrow foothills; and then behind the city there rose the Pagos, a hill covered with temples and noble buildings which were spoken of as "The Crown of

Smyrna." A modern traveller describes it as "a queenly city crowned with towers." Aristides likened Smyrna to a great statue with the feet in the sea; the middle parts in the plain and the foothills; and the head, crowned with great buildings, on the Pagos behind. He called it "a flower of beauty such as earth and sun had never showed to mankind."

Its history had not a little to do with the beauty of Smyrna, for it was one of the very few planned cities in the world. It had been founded as a Greek colony as far back as 1000 B.C. Round about 600 B.C. disaster had befallen it, for then the Lydians had broken in from the east and destroyed it. For four hundred years Smyrna had been no city, but a collection of little villages; then Lysimachus had rebuilt it as a planned whole. It was built with great, straight, broad streets. Strabo speaks of the handsomeness of the streets, the excellence of the paving and the great rectangular blocks in which it was built. Most famous of all the streets was the Street of Gold, which began with the Temple of Zeus and ended with the Temple of Cybele. It ran cross-wise across the foothills of the Pagos; and, if the buildings which encircled the Pagos were the crown of Smyrna, the Street of Gold was the necklace round the hill.

Here we have an interesting and a significant thing which shows the care and knowledge with which John set down his letters from the Risen Christ. The Risen Christ is called, "He who died and came to life." That was an echo of the experience of Smyrna itself.

Smyrna had other claims to greatness besides its city. It was a free city and it knew what loyalty was. Long before Rome was undisputed mistress of the world, Smyrna had cast in its lot with her, never to waver in its fidelity. Cicero called Smyrna "one of our most faithful and our most ancient allies." In the campaign against Mithradates in the far east things had gone badly with Rome. And when the soldiers of Rome were suffering from hunger and cold, the people of Smyrna stripped off their own clothes to send to them.

Such was the reverence of Smyrna for Rome that as far

back as 195 B.C. it was the first city in the world to erect a
temple to the goddess Roma. And in A.D. 26, when the cities
of Asia Minor were competing for the privilege of erecting a
temple to the godhead of Tiberius, Smyrna was picked out for
that honour, overcoming even Ephesus.

Not only was Smyrna great in trade, in beauty, in political
and in religious eminence; it was also a city where culture
flourished. Apollonius of Tyana had urged upon Smyrna the
truth that only men can make a city great. He said: "Though
Smyrna is the most beautiful of all cities under the sun, and
makes the sea its own, and holds the fountains of the zephyr,
yet it is a greater charm to wear a crown of men than a
crown of porticoes and pictures and gold beyond the standard of mankind: for buildings are seen only in their own
place, but men are seen everywhere and spoken about everywhere and make their city as vast as the range of countries
which they can visit." So Smyrna had a stadium in which
famous games were yearly held; a magnificent public library;
an Odeion which was the home of music; a theatre which
was one of the largest in Asia Minor. In particular, Smyrna was
one of the cities which laid claim to being the birthplace of
Homer; it had a memorial building called the Homereion
and put Homer's head on its coinage. This was a disputed
claim. Thomas Heywood, the seventeenth century poet, wrote
the famous epigram:

> Seven cities warr'd for Homer, being dead,
> Who, living, had no roof to shroud his head.

In such a city we would expect magnificent architecture, and
in Smyrna there was a host of temples, to Cybele, to Zeus,
to Apollo, to the Nemeseis, to Aphrodite, and to Asclepios.

Smyrna had rather more than its share of a characteristic
which was common to all Greek cities. Mommsen said that
Asia Minor was "a paradise of municipal vanity", and Smyrna
of all cities was noted for "its municipal rivalry and its local
pride." Everyone in it wished to exalt Smyrna and wished
himself to climb to the top of the municipal tree. It is not

without point that in the address of the letter the Risen Christ is called "the first and the last." In comparison with his glory all earthly distinctions are worthless.

There remains one feature of Smyrna which stands out in the letter and which had serious consequences for the Christians there. The Jews were specially numerous and influential (verse 9). We find them, for instance, contributing 10,000 *denarii* for the beautification of the city. It is clear that in Smyrna they were specially hostile to the Christian Church, no doubt because it was from them and from those interested in Judaism that Christianity drew many of its converts. So, then, we may well end this study of Smyrna with the story of the most famous Christian martyrdom which happened there.

Polycarp, Bishop of Smyrna, was martyred on Saturday, 23rd February, A.D. 155. It was the time of the public·games; the city was crowded; and the crowds were excited. Suddenly the shout went up: "Away with the atheists; let Polycarp be searched for." No doubt Polycarp could have escaped; but already he had had a dream vision in which he saw the pillow under his head burning with fire and he had awakened to tell his disciples: "I must be burnt alive."

His whereabouts was betrayed by a slave who collapsed under torture. They came to arrest him. He ordered that they should be given a meal and provided with all they wished, while he asked for himself the privilege of one last hour in prayer. Not even the police captain wished to see Polycarp die. On the brief journey to the city, he pled with the old man: "What harm is it to say, 'Caesar is Lord' and to offer sacrifice and be saved?" But Polycarp was adamant that for him only Jesus Christ was Lord.

When he entered the arena there came a voice from heaven saying: "Be strong, Polycarp, and play the man." The proconsul gave him the choice of cursing the name of Christ and making sacrifice to Caesar or death. "Eighty and six years have I served him," said Polycarp, "and he has done me no wrong. How can I blaspheme my King who saved me?"

The proconsul threatened him with burning, and Polycarp replied: "You threaten me with the fire that burns for a time, and is quickly quenched, for you do not know the fire which awaits the wicked in the judgment to come and in everlasting punishment. Why are you waiting? Come, do what you will."

So the crowds came flocking with faggots from the workshops and from the baths, and the Jews, even although they were breaking the Sabbath law by carrying such burdens, were foremost in bringing wood for the fire. They were going to bind him to the stake. "Leave me as I am," he said, "for he who gives me power to endure the fire, will grant me to remain in the flames unmoved even without the security you will give by the nails." So they left him loosely bound in the flames, and Polycarp prayed his great prayer:

O Lord God Almighty, Father of thy beloved and blessed Child, Jesus Christ, through whom we have received full knowledge of thee, God of angels and powers, and of all creation, and of the whole family of the righteous, who live before thee, I bless thee that thou hast granted unto me this day and hour, that I may share, among the number of the martyrs, in the cup of thy Christ, for the resurrection to eternal life, both of soul and body in the immortality of the Holy Spirit. And may I today be received among them before thee, as a rich and acceptable sacrifice, as thou, the God without falsehood and of truth, hast prepared beforehand and shown forth and fulfilled. For this reason I also praise thee for all things. I bless thee, I glorify thee through the eternal and heavenly High Priest, Jesus Christ, thy beloved Child, through whom be glory to thee with him and the Holy Spirit, both now and for the ages that are to come. Amen.

So much is plain fact, but then the story drifts into legend, for it goes on to tell that the flames made a kind of tent around Polycarp and left him untouched. At length the executioner stabbed him to death to achieve what the flames could not do. "And when he did this there came out a dove, and much blood, so that the fire was quenched, and all the crowd marvelled that there was such a difference between the unbelievers and the elect."

What is sure is that Polycarp died, a martyr for the faith.

It can have been no easy engagement to be a Christian at Smyrna, and yet the letter to Smyrna is one of the two in which there is undiluted praise.

SMYRNA
UNDER TRIAL

Revelation 2: 8–11 (*continued*)

THE Church of Smyrna was in trouble and further trial was imminent.

There are three things that the letter says about this trial.

(i) It is *thlipsis, affliction. Thlipsis* originally meant crushing beneath a weight. The pressure of events is on the Church at Smyrna.

(ii) It is *ptōcheia, poverty.* In the New Testament poverty and Christianity are closely connected. "Blessed are you poor," said Jesus (*Luke* 6: 20). Paul described the Christians at Corinth as being poor yet making many rich (2 *Corinthians* 6: 10). James speaks of God choosing the poor in this world to be rich in faith (*James* 2: 5).

In Greek there are two words for *poverty. Penia* describes the state of the man who is not wealthy and who, as the Greeks defined it, must satisfy his needs with his own hands. *Ptōcheia* describes complete destitution. It has been put this way—*penia* describes the state of the man who has nothing superfluous; *ptōcheia* describes the state of the man who has nothing at all.

The poverty of the Christians was due to two things. It was due to the fact that most of them belonged to the lower classes of society. The gulf between the top and the bottom of the social scale was very wide. We know, for instance, that in Rome the poorer classes literally starved because contrary winds delayed the corn ships from Alexandria and the corn dole could not be distributed.

There was another reason for the poverty of the Christians.

Sometimes they suffered from the spoiling of their goods (*Hebrews* 10: 4). There were times when the heathen mob would suddenly attack the Christians and wreck their homes. Life was not easy for a Christian in Smyrna or anywhere else in the ancient world.

(iii) There is *imprisonment*. John forecasts an imprisonment of *ten days*. That is not to be taken literally. *Ten days* was an expression for a short time which was soon to come to an end. So this prophecy is at once a warning and a promise. Imprisonment is coming, but the time of trouble, although sharp, will be short. Two things are to be noted.

First, this is exactly the way in which persecution came. To be a Christian was against the law, but persecution was not continuous. The Christians might be left in peace for a long time, but at any moment a governor might acquire a fit of administrative energy or the mob might set up a shout to find the Christians—and then the storm burst. The terror of being a Christian was the uncertainty.

Second, imprisonment does not sound so bad to us. We might say: "Imprisonment? Well, that is not so bad as death anyway." But in the ancient world imprisonment was merely the prelude to death. A man was only a prisoner until he was led out to die.

SMYRNA
THE CAUSE OF THE TROUBLE

Revelation 2: 8–11 (*continued*)

THE instigators of persecution were the Jews. Again and again in *Acts* we see how the Jews stirred up the authorities against the Christian preachers. It happened at Antioch (*Acts* 13: 50); at Iconium (*Acts* 14: 2, 5); at Lystra (*Acts* 14: 19); at Thessalonica (*Acts* 17: 5).

The story of what happened at Antioch shows us how the Jews often succeeded in moving the authorities to take action against the Christians (*Acts* 13: 50). Round the Jewish synagogues gathered many "god-fearers." These were Gentiles who were not prepared to go the whole way and to become proselytes but they were attracted by the preaching of one God instead of many gods, and were attracted specially by the purity of the Jewish ethic as compared with the heathen life. In particular women were attracted to Judaism for these reasons. Often these women were of high station, the wives of magistrates and governors, and it was through them that the Jews got at the authorities and moved them to persecute.

John calls the Jews the *synagogue of Satan*. He is taking a favourite expression of the Jews and reversing it. When the people of Israel met together they loved to call themselves "the assembly of the Lord" (*Numbers* 16: 3; 20: 4; 31: 16). *Synagogue* is in Greek *sunagōgē,* which literally means a coming together, an assembly, a congregation. It is as if John said: "You call yourselves the assembly of God when, in fact, you are the assembly of the devil." Once John Wesley said of certain men who were presenting a crude picture of God: "Your God is my devil." It is a terrible thing when religion becomes the means of evil things. It has happened. In the days of the French Revolution, Madame Roland uttered her famous cry: "Liberty, what crimes are committed in your name!" There have been tragic times when the same could be said about religion.

Six slanders were regularly levelled against the Christians.

(i) On the basis of the words of the Sacrament—this is my body, and this is my blood—the story went about that the Christians were cannibals.

(ii) Because the Christians called their common meal the *Agapē,* the Love Feast, it was said that their gatherings were orgies of lust.

(iii) Because Christianity did, in fact, often split families, when some members became Christians and some did not, the Christians were accused of "tampering with family relationships."

(iv) The heathen accused the Christians of atheism because they could not understand a worship which had no images of the gods such as they themselves had.

(v) The Christians were accused of being politically disloyal because they would not say: "Caesar is Lord."

(vi) The Christians were accused of being incendiaries because they foretold the end of the world in flames.

It was not difficult for maliciously-minded people to disseminate dangerous slanders about the Christian Church.

SMYRNA
CHRIST'S CLAIM AND CHRIST'S DEMAND

Revelation 2: 8–11 (*continued*)

WE have seen that the Church at Smyrna was battling with difficulties and threatened with worse to come. In view of that the letter to Smyrna opens with two resounding titles of Christ which tell what he can offer to a man confronted with such a situation as faced the Christians at Smyrna.

(i) Christ is the first and the last. In the old Testament that is a title belonging to God. "I am the first," Isaiah heard God say, "and I am the last" (*Isaiah* 44: 6; 48: 12). This title has two aspects. To the Christian it is a tremendous promise. Come what will, from the first day of life to the last the Risen Christ is with us. Of whom then shall we be afraid?

But to the pagans of Smyrna it was a warning. They loved their city calling it the first in Asia, and they themselves were all striving every man to be one better than his neighbours. The Risen Christ said: "I am the first and the last." Here is the death of human pride. Beside the glory of Christ all human titles are of no importance and all human claims become ridiculous. When Julian, the Roman Emperor, had failed in his attempt to banish Christianity and bring back the old gods, and when he had come to death in the attempt, he said: "To shoulder Christ from out the topmost niche was not for me."

(ii) Christ is he who was dead and is alive again. The tenses of the verb are of the first importance. The Greek for *was* is *genomenos,* which means *became.* It describes what we might call a passing phase. Christ became dead; it was episode through which he passed. In the Greek the verb which the Authorized Version translates *is alive* is not a present tense but an aorist, which describes one action completed in the past. The right translation is *came to life again* (as in the Revised Standard Version), and the reference is to the event of the Resurrection. The Risen Christ is he who experienced death came to life again in the triumphant event of the Resurrection, and is alive for evermore. Here again there are two aspects.

(*a*) The Risen Christ is one who has *experienced* the worst that life could do to him. He had died in the agony of the Cross. No matter what happened to the Christians of Smyrna, Jesus Christ had been through it. Jesus Christ can help because he knows what life is like at its worst and has experienced even the bitterness of death.

(*b*) The Risen Christ has *conquered* the worst that life can do. He triumphed over pain and over death; and he offers us through himself the way to victorious living.

In this passage there is also a demand, and the demand is for *loyalty,* loyal even when death is the price to be paid. Loyalty was a quality of which the people of Smyrna knew something, for their city had flung in its lot with Rome, when Rome's greatness was only a far off possibility, and had never wavered from in its allegiance, in fair weather and in foul. If all the other noble qualities of life were placed in the balance against it, loyalty would outweigh them all. It was R. L. Stevenson's prayer that "in all the chances of fortune, and down to the gates of death" we should be "loyal and loving to one another."

SMYRNA
THE PROMISED REWARD

Revelation 2: 8–11 (*continued*)

Jesus Christ will be in no man's debt and loyalty to him brings its own reward. In this passage two rewards are mentioned.

(i) There is *the crown of life*. Again and again the crown of the Christian is mentioned in the New Testament. Here and in *James* 1: 12 it is the crown of *life*. Paul speaks of the crown of *righteousness* (2 *Timothy* 4: 8), and of the crown of *boasting* (1 *Thessalonians* 2: 19). Peter speaks of the crown of *glory* (1 *Peter* 5: 4). Paul contrasts the immortal crown of the Christian with the fading crown of laurel which was the prize of the victor in the games (1 *Corinthians* 9: 25), and Peter speaks of the unfading crown of glory (1 *Peter* 5: 4).

Of in each of these phrases means *which consists of*. To win the crown of righteousness or glory or life is to be crowned with righteousness or glory or with life. But we must understand the idea behind this word *crown* (*stephanos*). In Greek there are two words for *crown*, *diadēma*, which means the *royal crown*, and *stephanos,* which has usually something to do with *joy* and *victory*. It is not the royal crown which is being offered to the Christian; it is the crown of joy and victory. *Stephanos* has many associations, and all of them contribute something to the riches of thought behind it.

(*a*) First to the mind comes the victor's crown in the games. Smyrna had games which were famous all over Asia. As in the Olympic Games, the reward of the victorious athlete was the laurel crown. The Christian can win the crown of victory in the contest of life.

(*b*) When a man had faithfully performed the work of a magistrate, at the end of his term of office he was granted a crown. He who throughout life faithfully serves Christ and his fellow-men will receive his crown.

(*c*) The heathen world was in the habit of wearing crowns, chaplets of flowers, at banquets. At the end of the day, if the Christian is loyal, he will have the joy of sitting as a guest at the banquet of God.

(*d*) The heathen worshippers were in the habit of wearing crowns when they approached the temples of their gods. At the end of the day, if he has been faithful, the Christian will have the joy of entering into the nearer presence of God.

(*e*) Some scholars have seen in this crown a reference to the halo or the nimbus which is round the head of divine beings in pictures. If that is so, it means that the Christian, if he is faithful, will be crowned with the life which belongs to God himself. As John said: "We shall be like him, for we shall see him as he is" (1 *John* 3: 2).

In this life it may be that the Christian's loyalty will bring him a crown of thorns, but in the life to come it will surely bring him the crown of glory.

(ii) Cyprian uses two great phrases to describe those who are faithful unto death. He describes them as "illustrious with the heraldry of a good name," and he calls them "the white-robed cohort of the soldiers of Christ." To the faithful another promise is made: they will not be hurt by the *second death*. The *second death* is a mysterious phrase which occurs nowhere in the New Testament outside the *Revelation* (20: 6, 14; 21: 8). The Rabbis talked of "the second death whereof the wicked die in the next world." The phrase may have two origins.

(*a*) The Sadducees believed that after death there was absolutely nothing; the Epicureans held the same doctrine. This belief finds its place even in the Old Testament for that pessimistic book *Ecclesiastes* is the work of a Sadducee. "A living dog is better than a dead lion; for the living know that they will die, but the dead know nothing" (*Ecclesiastes* 9: 4, 5). For the Sadducees and the Epicureans death was extinction. To the orthodox Jew this was too easy, for it meant that for the wise and for the fool the end was the same (*Ecclesiastes* 2: 15, 16; 9: 2). They, therefore, came to believe that there were, so to speak, two deaths—physical death which every man must undergo and after that a death which was the judgment of God.

(*b*) This is very closely connected with the ideas which we touched on when studying the word *paradise* (2: 7). We saw that many of the Jews and the early Christian thinkers believed that there was an intermediate state into which all men passed until the time of judgment. If that were so, then indeed there would be two deaths, the physical death which no man can escape and the spiritual death into which the wicked would enter after the final judgment.

Of such things it is not given to any man to speak with confidence but, when John spoke of the faithful being unharmed by the second death, he meant precisely the same as Paul when he said that nothing in life or in death, in time or in eternity can separate those who love him from Jesus Christ. Such a man is safe from all that life or death can do to him (*Romans* 8: 38, 39).

THE LETTER TO PERGAMUM

Revelation 2: 12–17

And to the angel of the Church in Pergamum, write:

These things says he who has the sharp two-edged sword.
I know where your home is. I know that it is where the throne of Satan is; and yet you hold fast to my name, and have not denied your loyalty to me, even in the days of Antipas, my faithful martyr, who was killed among you, where Satan has his home. But I have a few things against you. You have among you some people who hold the teaching of Balaam, who taught Balak to put a stumbling-block before the children of Israel, to eat meat offered to idols and to commit fornication. So you, too, have those who in the same way hold the teaching of the Nicolaitans. So, then, repent. If you do not, I am coming to you quickly, and I will go to war with them with the sword of my mouth.
Let him who has an ear hear what the Spirit is saying to the Churches. To him who overcomes I will give a share of the hidden manna; and I will give him a white stone, and written on the stone a new name, which no one but him who receives it knows.

PERGAMUM
THE SEAT OF SATAN

Revelation 2: 12–17

THERE is a difference in the name of this city in the different translations of the New Testament. The Authorized Version calls it *Pergamos,* while the Revised Version, the Revised Standard Version and Moffat call it *Pergamum. Pergamos* is the feminine form of the name and *Pergamum* the neuter. In the ancient world it was known by both forms but *Pergamum* was much the commoner and the newer translations are right to prefer it.

Pergamum had a place all its own in Asia. It was not on any of the great roads, as Ephesus and Smyrna were, but historically it was the greatest city in Asia. Strabo called it an illustrious (*epiphanēs*) city and Pliny called it "by far the most famous city in Asia" (*longe clarissimum Asiae*). The reason was that, by the time John was writing, Pergamum had been a capital city for almost four hundred years. Back in 282 B.C. it was made the capital of the Seleucid kingdom, one of the sections into which the empire of Alexander the Great was broken up. It remained the capital until 133 B.C. In that year Attalus the Third died and before he died he willed his dominions into the possession of Rome. Out of the dominions of Attalus, Rome formed the province of Asia and Pergamum still remained its capital.

Its geographical position made Pergamum even more impressive. It was built on a tall conical hill, which dominated the valley of the River Caicus, from the top of which the Mediterranean could be seen, fifteen miles away. Sir William Ramsay describes it: "Beyond all other cities in Asia Minor, it gives the traveller the impression of a royal city, the home of authority; the rocky hill on which it stands is so huge, and dominates the broad plain of the Caicus so proudly and so boldly." History and honour gathered around Pergamum. Let us then set down its outstanding characteristics.

(i) Pergamum could never achieve the commercial greatness of Ephesus or of Smyrna but it was a centre of culture which surpassed both. It was famous for its library, which contained no fewer than 200,000 parchment rolls. It was second only to the unique library of Alexandria.

It is interesting to note that the word *parchment* is derived from *Pergamum*. In the ancient world *parchment* was *hē pergamēnē charta, the Pergamene sheet*; and to this name attaches a story. For many centuries ancient rolls were written on papyrus, a substance made of the pith of a very large bulrush which grows beside the Nile. The pith was extracted, cut into strips, pressed into sheets and smoothed. There emerged a substance not unlike brown paper, and this was universally used for writing. In the third century B.C. a Pergamene king called Eumenēs was very anxious to make the library of the city supreme. In order to do so he persuaded Aristophanes of Byzantium, the librarian at Alexandria, to agree to leave Alexandria and come to Pergamum. Ptolemy of Egypt, enraged at this seduction of his outstanding scholar, promptly imprisoned Aristophanes and by way of retaliation put an embargo on the export of papyrus to Pergamum. Faced with this situation, the scholars of Pergamum invented parchment or vellum, which is made of the skins of beasts, smoothed and polished. In fact parchment is a much superior vehicle for writing and, although it did not do so for many centuries, it in the end ousted papyrus altogether as writing material.

(ii) Pergamum was one of the great religious centres. In particular it had two famous shrines. In the letter of the Risen Christ Pergamum is said to be the place where "Satan's seat" is. Obviously this must refer to something which the Christian Church regarded as particularly evil. Some have found the reference explained in Pergamum's religious splendour.

(*a*) Pergamum regarded itself as the custodian of the Greek way of life and of the Greek worship. About 240 B.C. it had won a great victory against the savage invading Galatae or

Gauls. In memory of that victory a great altar to Zeus was
built in front of the Temple of Athene which stood eight
hundred feet up on Pergamum's conical hill. Forty feet high,
it stood on a projecting ledge of rock and looked exactly like
a great throne on the hillside. All day it smoked with the
smoke of sacrifices offered to Zeus. Around its base was
carved one of the greatest achievements in the world of sculp-
ture, the frieze which showed the Battle of the Giants, in which
the gods of Greece were victorious over the giants of the
barbarians. It has been suggested that this great altar was
Satan's seat. But it is unlikely that a Christian writer would
call that altar Satan's seat, for even by this time the old
Greek gods were anachronisms and it would have been a waste
of the powder and shot of Christian invective to attack them.

(b) Pergamum was particularly connected with the worship
of Asclepios, so much so that Asclepios was known as "the
Pergamene god." When Galen was mentioning favourite
oaths, he said that people commonly swore by Artemis of
Ephesus, or Apollo of Delphi, or Asclepios of Pergamum.
Asclepios was the god of healing and his temples were the
nearest approach to hospitals in the ancient world. From all
over the world people flocked to Pergamum for relief for
their sicknesses. R. H. Charles has called Pergamum "the
Lourdes of the ancient world." The task of healing was partly
the work of the priests; partly the work of doctors—Galen,
second only to Hippocrates in the medical history of the
ancient world, was born in Pergamum; and partly the work
of Asclepios himself. Was there anything in that worship to
move the Christians to call the Temple of Asclepios Satan's
seat? There may have been two things.

First, the commonest and most famous title for Asclepios
was *Asclepios Sōtēr*, Asclepios the Saviour. It might well be
that the Christians felt a shudder of horror that the name
Saviour should be given to anyone other than Jesus Christ,
the Saviour of the world.

Second, the emblem of Asclepios was the serpent, which
still appears on the cap badge of the Royal Army Medical

Corps. Many of the coins of Pergamum have Asclepios's serpent as part of their design. It might well be that Jew or Christian might regard a religion which took the serpent as its emblem as a Satanic cult. Again this explanation seems unlikely. As has been pointed out, the Christians would regard the place where men went to be healed—and often were—with pity rather than with indignation. The worship of Asclepios surely would not give adequate ground for calling Pergamum Satan's seat.

It seems then that we must look elsewhere for the explanation of this phrase.

(iii) Pergamum was the administrative centre of Asia. That meant that it was the centre of Caesar worship for the province. We have already described Caesar worship and the dire dilemma in which it placed the Christian (pp 15–20).

It was organized with a provincial centre and an administration like that of a presbytery or diocese. The point here is that Pergamum was the centre of that worship for the province of Asia. Undoubtedly that is why Pergamum was Satan's seat; it was the place where men were required on pain of death to take the name of *Lord* and give it to Caesar instead of to Christ; and to a Christian there could be nothing more Satanic than that.

And here is the explanation of the beginning of the letter to Pergamum. The Risen Christ is called *he who has the sharp two-edged sword.* Roman governors were divided into two classes—those who had the *ius gladii,* the right of the sword, and those who had not. Those who had the right of the sword had the power of life and death; on their word a man could be executed on the spot. Humanly speaking the proconsul, who had his headquarters at Pergamum, had the *ius gladii,* the right of the sword, and at any moment he might use it against any Christian; but the letter bids the Christian not to forget that the last word is still with the Risen Christ, who has the sharp two-edged sword. The power of Rome might be satanically powerful; the power of the Risen Lord is greater yet.

PERGAMUM
AN ENGAGEMENT VERY DIFFICULT

Revelation 2: 12–17 (*continued*)

To be a Christian in Pergamum was to face what Cromwell would have called "an engagement very difficult."

We have already seen what a concentration of pagan religion had its centre in Pergamum. There was the worship of Athene and Zeus, with its magnificent altar dominating the city; there was the worship of Asclepios, bringing sick people from far and near; and above all there were the demands of Caesar worship, hanging for ever like a poised sword above the heads of the Christians.

So the Risen Christ says to the Christians of Pergamum: "I know where you stay." The word for *to stay* is here *katoikein*; and it means to have one's permanent residence in a place. It is a very unusual word to use of Christians in the world. Usually the word used of them is *paroikein*, which means to be a sojourner. Peter writes his letter to the *sojourners* throughout the provinces of Asia Minor. But here the matter is being regarded from another point of view. The Christians of Pergamum have their permanent residence, so far as this world is concerned, in Pergamum; and Pergamum is the place where Satan's rule is strongest.

Here is something very important. The principle of the Christian life is not escape, but conquest. We may feel it would be very much easier to be a Christian in some other place and in some other circumstances but the duty of the Christian is to witness for Christ where life has set him. We once heard of a girl who was converted in an evangelistic campaign. A reporter on a secular newspaper, her first step after her conversion was to get a new job on a small Christian newspaper where she was constantly in the society of professing Christians. It was strange that the first thing that her conversion did was to make her run away. The more difficult it is to be a Christian in any set of circumstances, the greater the obligation to remain within these circumstances. If in the early days Christians had run away every time they were confronted with a difficult engagement, there would have been no chance of a world for Christ.

The Christians at Pergamum proved that it was perfectly possible to be a Christian under such circumstances. Even when martyrdom was in the air they did not flinch. Of Antipas we know nothing; there is a late legend in Tertullian that he met his death by being slowly roasted to death within a brazen bull. But there is a point in the Greek impossible to reproduce in English which is intensely suggestive. The Risen Christ calls Antipas my faithful *martus*. We have translated that *martyr*; but *martus* is the normal Greek word for *witness*. In the early church to be a martyr and to be a witness were one and the same thing. *Witness* meant so often *martyrdom*. Here is a rebuke to us. So many are prepared to demonstrate their Christianity in Christian circles but are equally prepared to play it down in circles where Christianity is met with opposition.

We must note another thing. The Risen Christ calls Antipas *my faithful martus* and so gives him nothing less than his own title. In *Revelation* 1: 5 and 3: 14 Christ himself is called *the faithful martus*; to those who are true to him he gives nothing less than his own name.

PERGAMUM
THE DOOM OF ERROR

Revelation 2: 12–17 (*continued*)

IN spite of the fidelity of the Church at Pergamum there is error. There are those who hold the teaching of Balaam and the doctrine of the Nicolaitans. We have already discussed these people in connection with Ephesus and we meet them again when we come to study the letter of Thyatira. They sought to persuade Christians that there was nothing wrong with a prudent conformity to the world's standards.

The man who is not prepared to be different need not start on the Christian way at all. The commonest word for the Christian in the New Testament is *hagios* whose basic meaning is *different* or *separate*. The Temple is *hagios* because it is *different* from other buildings; the Sabbath day is *hagios* because it is different from other days; God is supremely *hagios* because he is totally different from men; and the Christian is *hagios* because he is different from other men.

We must be clear what this difference means, for there is a paradox in it. It is Paul's summons to the Corinthians that they should be different from the world. "Come out from among them" (2 *Corinthians* 6: 17). This difference from the world does not involve separation from it nor hatred for it. Paul says in writing to the very same Church: "I have become all things to all men, that I might by all means save some" (1 *Corinthians* 9: 22). It was Paul's claim that he could get alongside all men; but—and here is the point—his getting alongside them was *that he might save some*. It was not a question of bringing Christianity down to their level; it was a question of bringing them up. The fault of the Nicolaitans was that they were following a policy of compromise solely to save themselves from trouble.

It is the word of the Risen Christ that he will make war with them. We must note that he did not say: "I will go to war with *you*"; he said: "I will go to war with *them*." His wrath was not directed against the whole Church but against those who were seducing her; for those who were led astray, he had nothing but pity.

It is the threat of the Risen Christ that he will make war against them with *the sword of his mouth*. The Christ of the sword is a startling idea. Thinking of past conquerors and comparing them with Jesus Christ, the poet wrote:

> Then all these vanished from the scene,
> Like flickering shadows on a glass;
> And conquering down the centuries came
> The swordless Christ upon an ass.

What then is the sword of Christ? The writer to the Hebrews speaks of the word of God which is sharper than any two-edged sword (*Hebrews* 4: 12). Paul speaks of "the sword of the Spirit which is the word of God" (*Ephesians* 6: 17). The sword of Christ is the word of Christ.

In the word of Christ there is *conviction of sin*; in it a man is confronted with the truth and thereby with his own failure to obey it. In the word of Christ there is *invitation to God*; it convicts a man of sin and then invites him back to the love of God. In the word of Christ there is *assurance of salvation*; it convicts a man of sin, it leads him to the Cross, and it assures him that there is no other name under heaven given among men by which we must be saved (*Acts* 4: 12). The conquest of Christ is his power to win men to the love of God.

PERGAMUM
THE BREAD OF HEAVEN

Revelation 2: 12-17 (*continued*)

In this letter the Risen Christ promises two things to the man who overcomes; the first is a share of the *hidden manna* to eat. Here is a Jewish conception which has two aspects.

(i) When the children of Israel had no food in the desert God gave them manna to eat (*Exodus* 16: 11-15). When the need of the manna passed, the memory did not. A pot of the manna was put into the ark and laid up before God in the Holy of Holies in the tabernacle and in the Temple (*Exodus* 16: 33, 34; *Hebrews* 9: 4). Early in the sixth century B.C. the Temple which Solomon had built was destroyed; and the rabbis had a legend that, when that happened, Jeremiah hid away the pot of manna in a cleft in Mount Sinai and that, when the Messiah came, he would return and the pot of manna would be discovered again. To a Jew "to eat of the hidden manna" meant to enjoy the blessings of the Messianic age. To a Christian it meant to enter into the blessedness of the new world which would emerge when the Kingdom came.

(ii) There may be a wider and more general meaning. Of the manna it is said: "This is the bread which the Lord has given you to eat" (*Exodus* 16: 15). The manna is called "grain of heaven" (*Psalm* 78: 24); and it is said to be the "bread of the angels," (*Psalm* 78: 25). Here the manna may mean *heavenly food.* In that case John would be saying: "In this world you cannot share with the heathen in their feasts because you cannot sit down to meat which is part of a sacrifice that has been offered to an idol. You may think that you are being called upon to give up much but the day will come when you will feast in heaven upon heavenly food." If that is so, the Risen Christ is saying that a man must abstain from the seductions of earth if he wishes to enjoy the blessings of heaven.

(iii) There is one possible further interpretation of this. Some have suggested that the hidden manna is the bread of God given to the Christian at the sacrament of the Lord's Supper. John tells us that when the Jews said to him that their fathers had eaten manna in the wilderness, so receiving bread, and Jesus said "I am the bread of life" (*John* 6: 31–35). If the hidden manna and the bread of life are the same, the hidden manna is not only the bread of the sacrament but stands for nothing less than Christ, the bread of life; and this is a promise that to him who is faithful he will give himself.

PERGAMUM
THE WHITE STONE AND THE NEW NAME

Revelation 2: 12–17 (*continued*)

THE final promise of Christ to the faithful in Pergamum is that he will give them the white stone with the new name on it. This is a passage of which there are almost endless interpretations. In the ancient world a white stone might stand for many things.

(i) There was a Rabbinic legend that precious stones fell from heaven along with the manna. The white stone would then simply stand for the precious gifts of God to his people.

(ii) In the ancient world coloured stones were used as counters for working out calculations. This would mean that the Christian is counted among the number of the faithful.

(iii) In the ancient law courts white and black stones were used for registering the verdict of juries, black for condemnation, white for acquittal. This would mean that the Christian is acquitted in the sight of God because of the work of Jesus Christ.

(iv) In the ancient world objects called *tesserae* were much used. A *tessera* was a little tablet made of wood or metal or stone; it had writing on it; and, generally speaking, the possession of a *tessera* conferred some kind of privilege upon a man. Three of these *tesserae* add something to the picture.

(*a*) In Rome the great houses had their *clients*, dependents who every morning received from their patron food and money for the day. They were often given a *tessera* by which they identified themselves as having the right to the free gifts. This would mean that the Christian has the right to the free gifts for life which Christ can give.

(*b*) To win a victory at the games was one of the greatest honours the ancient world could give. Outstanding victors were given, by the master of the games, a *tessera* which in the days to come conferred upon them the right of free entry to all public spectacles. This would mean that the Christian is the victorious athlete of Christ who is a sharer in the glory of his Lord.

(*c*) In Rome a great gladiator was the admired hero of all. Often a gladiator had to fight on until he was killed in combat. But if he had had a specially illustrious career, when he grew old, he was allowed to retire in honour. Such men were given a *tessera* with the letters SP on it. SP stands for the Latin word *spectatus,* which means a *man whose valour has been proved beyond a doubt*. This would mean that the Christian is the gladiator of Christ and that, when he has proved his valour in the battle of life, he is allowed to enter into the rest which Christ gives with honour.

(v) In the ancient world a specially happy day was called *a white day*. Plutarch tells that when Pericles was besieging Samos he knew that the siege would be long; he did not wish his army to grow weary; so he divided it into eight parts; every day the eight companies drew lots; one was a white bean; and the company which drew the white bean was exempt from duty for the day and could enjoy itself as it wished. So it was that a happy day came to be called a white day (Plutarch: *Life of Pericles* 64). Pliny in one of his letters tells a friend that that day he had had the joy of hearing in the law courts two magnificent young pleaders in whose hands the future of Roman oratory was safe; and, he says, that experience made that day one marked *candidissimo calculo*, with the whitest of stones (Pliny: *Letters* 6: 11). It was said that the Thracians and the Scythians kept in their homes an urn into which for every happy day they threw a white stone and for every unhappy day a black stone; at the end of their lives the stones were counted, and as the white or the black preponderated, a man was said to have had a wretched or a happy life. This would mean that through Jesus Christ the Christian can have the joy that no man takes from him (*John* 16: 22).

(vi) Along this line there is another and most likely interpretation. One of the commonest of all customs in the ancient world was to carry an amulet or charm. It might be made of a precious metal or a precious stone but often it was nothing more than a pebble. On the pebble there was a sacred name; to know a god's name was to have a certain power over him, to be able to summon him to one's aid in time of difficulty and to have mastery over the demons. Such an amulet was thought to be doubly effective, if no one other than the owner knew the name that was inscribed upon it. Most likely what John is saying is: "Your heathen friends—and you did the same in your heathen days—carry amulets with superstitious inscriptions on them and they think they will keep them safe. You need nothing like that; you are safe in life and in death because you know the name of the only true God."

PERGAMUM
RENAMED BY GOD

Revelation 2: 12–17 (*continued*)

It is just possible that we ought to look for the meaning of the new name and the white stone in another direction altogether.

The words *white* and *new* are characteristic of the *Revelation*. R. H. Charles has said that in the *Revelation* "white is the colour and livery of heaven." The word used does not describe a dull, flat whiteness but one which glistens like snow in the winter sun. So in the *Revelation* we find white garments (3: 5); white robes (7: 9); white linen (19: 8, 14); and the great white throne of God himself (20: 11). White, then, is heaven's colour.

In Greek there are two words for *new*. There is *neos*, which means new in point of time. A thing can be *neos*, and yet exactly like any number of things. On the other hand there is *kainos*, which is new not only in point of time but also in point of quality; nothing like it has ever been made before. So in the *Revelation* there is the new Jerusalem (3: 12); the new song (5: 9); the new heavens and the new earth (21: 1); and God makes all things new (21: 5). With this in mind two lines of thought have been suggested.

It has been suggested that the white stone is the man himself; that the Risen Christ is promising his faithful ones a new self, cleansed of all earthly stains and glistening with the purity of heaven.

As to the new name, one of the features of the Old Testament is the giving to a man of a new name to mark a new status. So Abram becomes Abraham when the great promise is made that he will be the father of many nations and when he, as it were, acquires a new status in the plan of God for men (*Genesis* 17: 5). So after the wrestling at Peniel, Jacob becomes Israel, which means the prince of God, because he had prevailed with God (*Genesis* 32: 28). Isaiah hears the promise of God to the nation of Israel: "The nations shall see your vindication, and all the kings your glory; and you shall be called by a new name which the mouth of the Lord will give" (*Isaiah* 62: 2).

This custom of giving a new name to mark a new status was known in the heathen world as well. The name of the first of the Roman Emperors was Octavius; but when he became Emperor he was given the name Augustus to mark his new status.

A curious superstitious parallel to this comes from peasant life in Palestine. When a person was very ill and in danger of death, he was often given the name of someone who had lived a long and saintly life, as if this turned him into a new person over whom the illness might lose its power.

On this basis of interpretation, Christ promises a new status to those who are faithful to him.

This is attractive. It suggests that the white stone means that Jesus Christ gives to the man who is true to him a new self and that the new name means the new status of glory into which the man who has been true to Christ will enter when this life ends and when the next begins. It remains to say that, attractive as that interpretation is, the view which traces back the white stone and the new name to the use of amulets is more likely to be correct.

THE LETTER TO THYATIRA

Revelation 2: 18–29

And to the angel of the Church in Thyatira write:

These things says the Son of God, who has eyes like a flame of fire and whose feet are like beaten brass.

I know your works—I mean your love and your loyalty and your service and your steadfast endurance; and I know that your last works are more than your first.

But I hold it against you that you make no effort to deal with the woman Jezebel, who calls herself a prophetess and whose misleading teaching causes my servants to commit fornication and to eat meat offered to idols. I have given her a time within which to repent and she refuses to repent from her fornication. Behold, I am going to cast her into a bed and I am going to cast her paramours into great affliction, unless they repent from her deeds; and I will slay her children with death; and all the Churches will know that I am he who searches the inmost desires and thoughts of a man's being; and I will give to each one of you what your works deserve.

To the rest of you in Thyatira, to all those who do not hold this teaching, to such as have not known the depths of Satan, as they call them, I say this—I am not going to put any other burden on you. All I say is, hold on to what you have until I come.

I will give to him who overcomes, and who keeps my works to the end, authority over the Gentiles; and he will smite them with a rod of iron; like vessels of pottery they will be smashed; for this is the authority that I have received from my Father; and I will give him the morning star.

Let him who has an ear hear what the Spirit is saying to the Churches.

THYATIRA
THE PERIL OF COMPROMISE

Revelation 2: 18–29

THE longest of the seven letters is written to the least important of the seven cities. None the less, the problem which faced Thyatira and the danger which threatened it were those which were universally involved in the position of the Christians in Asia.

Thyatira lies in the long valley connecting the valleys of the Hermus and the Caicus rivers through which the railway runs today; and it was its geographical position which gave it its importance.

(i) Thyatira lay on the road which connected Pergamum with Sardis and went on to Philadelphia and to Laodicea, linking up with both Smyrna and Byzantium. That was the road by which the imperial post travelled; and it was crowded with the commerce of Asia and the east. Therefore, first and foremost Thyatira was a great commercial town.

(ii) Strategically the importance of Thyatira was that it was the gateway to Pergamum, the capital of the province. The first we hear of Thyatira is that it is an armed garrison, manned by a company of Macedonian troops, placed there as an outpost to protect Pergamum. The difficulty was that Thyatira was not capable of any prolonged defence. It lay in an open valley. There was no height that could be fortified; and all that Thyatira could ever hope to do was to fight a delaying action until Pergamum could prepare to meet the invaders.

(iii) Thyatira had no special religious significance. It was not a centre of either Caesar or of Greek worship. Its local hero-god was called Tyrimnus and he appears on its coins on horseback armed with battle-axe and club. The only notable thing about Thyatira from the religious point of view was that it possessed a fortune-telling shrine, presided over by a female oracle called the Sambathē. Certainly no threat of persecution hung over the Thyatiran Church.

(iv) What, then, was the problem in Thyatira? We know less about Thyatira than about any other of the seven cities and are, therefore, seriously handicapped in trying to reconstruct the situation. The one thing we do know is that it was a great commercial centre, specially of the dyeing industry and of the trade in woollen goods. It was from Thyatira that Lydia, the seller of purple, came (*Acts* 16: 14). From inscriptions discovered we learn that it had an extraordinary number of trade guilds. These were associations for mutual profit and pleasure of people employed in certain trades. There were guilds of workers in wool, leather, linen and bronze, makers of outer garments, dyers, potters, bakers and slave-dealers.

Here, we think, was the problem of the Church in Thyatira. To refuse to join one of these guilds would be much the same as to refuse to join a trade union today. It would mean to give up all prospect of commercial existence. Why should a Christian not join one of these guilds? They held common meals. These would very often be held in a temple and even if not, they would begin and end with a formal sacrifice to the gods, and the meat eaten would be meat which had already been offered to idols. Further, it often happened that these communal meals were occasions of drunken revelry and slack morality. Was it possible for a Christian to be part of such occasions?

Here was the problem at Thyatira; the threat came from inside the Church. There was a strong movement, led by the woman addressed as Jezebel, which pled for compromise with the world's standards in the interests of business and commercial prosperity, maintaining, no doubt, that the Holy Spirit could preserve them from any harm. The answer of the Risen Christ is unequivocal. With such things the Christian must have nothing to do.

THYATIRA
THE STATE OF THE CHURCH IN THYATIRA

Revelation 2: 18–29 (*continued*)

R. H. CHARLES points out that by far the longest of the seven letters is written to the most unimportant of the seven cities; but its problem was far from being unimportant.

Of all the seven letters this is the most enigmatic. Our trouble is that we have so little definite information about Thyatira and we are presented with a series of four questions —What was the situation of the Church in Thyatira? Who was Jezebel? What did she teach? What do the promises made to the Church at Thyatira mean?

(i) The letter opens with a description of the Risen Christ which has a threat in it. His eyes are like a flame of fire and his feet like burnished bronze. The description is taken from that of the angelic messenger in *Daniel* 10: 6: "His face was like the appearance of lightning, and his eyes like flaming torches, his arms and legs like the gleam of burnished bronze." The flaming eyes must stand for two things, blazing anger against sin and the awful penetration of that gaze which strips the disguises away and sees into a man's inmost heart. The brazen feet must stand for the immovable power of the Risen Christ. A message which begins like that will certainly be no soothing tranquillizer.

The letter goes on to terms of the highest praise. The love and loyalty and service and endurance of the Church at Thyatira are matters for congratulation. We must note how these great qualities go in pairs. Service is the outcome of love and patient endurance the product of loyalty.

Then comes the condemnation of the woman Jezebel and all her ways and teaching; and one can hardly avoid the conclusion that she had very considerable influence in the Church at Thyatira.

The necessary conclusion seems to be this. On the surface the Church at Thyatira was strong and flourishing. If a stranger went into it, he would be impressed with its abounding energy and its generous liberality and its apparent steadfastness. For all that, there was something essential missing.

Here is a warning. A church which is crowded with people and which is a hive of energy is not necessarily a real Church. It is possible for a Church to be crowded because its people come to be entertained instead of instructed, and to be soothed instead of confronted with the fact of sin and the offer of salvation; it may be a highly successful Christian club rather than a real Christian congregation.

THYATIRA
THE SOURCE OF THE ERROR

Revelation 18–29 (continued)

(2) THE source of the trouble in Thyatira centred round a woman whom the letter calls Jezebel. A variety of answers have been given to the question of her identity.

(i) We begin with an answer which is very interesting, although it is doubtful if it is possible. The Authorized Version calls her *that woman Jezebel*. Moffat translates "that Jezebel of a woman." The Greek is *tēn gunaika Iezebel*. A few manuscripts have after *gunaika* the word *sou*, which means *your*. The noun *gunē*—the nominative of the word of which *gunaika* is the accusative form—not only means *woman* but also *wife*; and if with these manuscripts we read *tēn gunaika sou Iezebel*, the phrase will mean *your wife Jezebel*.

Early on we saw that the *angel* of the Church may be the *bishop* of the Church. If, then, the letter is addressed to the bishop of the Church and there is a reference to *your wife Jezebel*, it means that the cause of all the trouble is the bishop's wife! That would be an interesting sidelight on the early Christian congregations and it would not be the last time that the wives of church officials were the sources of trouble in a congregation. But this interpretation must be rejected because the evidence for inserting *sou* is not good enough.

(ii) One of the few claims to distinction which Thyatira possessed was an oracle called the *Sambathē,* a woman fortune-teller. The Greeks made great use of oracles. The oracle at Delphi was world famous and the expression *a Delphic utterance* has become proverbial. It may be that this oracle was a Jewess, for the Jews in the ancient world went in largely for this business of fortune telling. There are those who see in the Sambathē the evil influence which was threatening the Church at Thyatira; but this, too, must be rejected, for it is quite clear that Jezebel was a member of the Church and her influence was being exerted from within.

(iii) Some, on no grounds whatever, have identified Jezebel with Lydia, the seller of purple from Thyatira, whom Paul met and converted at Philippi. It is suggested that she came back to Thyatira and became an evil influence in the Church because of her wealth and her business interests. That theory is merely a slander on Lydia.

(iv) The only reasonable conclusion is that we have no idea who Jezebel was, although we can with certainty trace the kind of person that she was.

That she claimed to be a prophetess is not so very surprising. It is true that Paul would have nothing to do with women speaking in the Church (1 *Corinthians* 14: 34). But it is also true that in both the Old and the New Testaments there are prophetesses. In the Old Testament there are Miriam (*Exodus* 15: 20), Deborah (*Judges* 4: 4) and Huldah (2 *Kings* 22: 14); and in the New Testament there are Anna (*Luke* 2: 36), and the four virgin daughters of Philip (*Acts* 21: 9).

This woman is called *Jezebel* and, therefore, her character must be discovered in the original Jezebel than whom few women have acquired such a reputation for wickedness. She was the daughter of Ethbaal, king of Sidon, and the wife of Ahab (1 *Kings* 16: 31). When she came from Sidon, she brought her own gods and caused Ahab and his people to worship Baal. It was not that she would have wished to banish the worship of Jehovah, if the prophets of Jehovah would have accepted Baal *in addition to* Jehovah. She slew the prophets of the Lord and at her own table supported four hundred and fifty prophets of Baal (1 *Kings* 18: 13, 19). She was Ahab's evil genius; in particular, she was responsible for the murder of Naboth in order that Ahab might enter into the possession of the ground where his vineyard stood (1 *Kings* 21). And she left behind her a name for "harlotries and sorceries" (2 *Kings* 9: 22).

All this must mean that Jezebel of Thyatira was an evil influence on the life and worship of the Christian Church. It must be clearly understood that she had no wish to destroy the Church; but she wished to bring into it new ways which were, in fact, destructive of the faith.

THYATIRA
THE TEACHING OF JEZEBEL (1)

Revelation 2: 18–29 (*continued*)

(3) THIS Jezebel of a woman is accused of teaching two things —eating meat offered to idols and committing fornication.

(*a*) One of the great problems of the Christian Church was that of meat offered to idols and it was one which met the Christian every day. When a man made a sacrifice in a Greek temple, very little of the meat was burned on the altar. Sometimes all that was actually burned was a few hairs cut from the forehead of the animal. The priests received a share of the meat of the animal as their perquisite; and the worshipper received the rest. With it he did one of two things. He might hold a feast of his friends within the temple precincts. A common form of invitation to a festal meal ran: "I invite you to dine with me at the table of our Lord Serapis." Or he might take the meat home and hold a feast in his own house. Here was the Christian problem. Could a Christian, in a temple or anywhere else, eat meat which had been consecrated to idols? Paul discusses this very problem in 1 *Corinthians* 8–10.

The problem was complicated by the fact that even the meat

in butchers' shops might well have been offered to idols pre-viously. The priests in the temples could not possibly consume all the meat which fell to them and therefore, sold much of their share to the butchers' shops. Such meat was the best meat. What was a Christian going to do about that?

The Church had no doubt as to where a Christian's duty lay. Abstention from things offered to idols was one of the conditions on which the Gentiles received the right of entry into the Christian Church (*Acts* 15: 29).

The prohibition of meat offered to idols had one far-reaching consequence. It came near to cutting off a Christian from all social fellowship with non-Christians; there were few social occasions, and almost no banquets, which he could share with the heathen world.

This had another consequence which, as we have already said, we think was at the back of the situation in Thyatira. It meant that the Christian could not join any trade guild for all the guilds had a common meal as a central part of their practice which might well be held in a heathen temple and would largely consist of meat offered to idols. His abstention from guild membership was equivalent to commercial suicide.

Here is where Jezebel came in. She urged upon the Christians that there was no need to cut themselves off from society or abstain from the guilds. When she did so, she was not pro-ceeding on grounds of principle but was simply trying to pro-tect her business interests. Jezebel is to be counted amongst those to whom the claims of commercial success speak more loudly than the claims of Christ.

THYATIRA
THE TEACHING OF JEZEBEL (2)

Revelation 2: 18–29 (*continued*)

(*b*) THE other part of Jezebel's teaching is not so clear. She is said to teach the people to commit fornication (verse 20); she is urged to repent from her fornication (verse 21); and her paramours and her children are threatened along with her (verses 22, 23). Is this reference to be taken literally or in the metaphorical sense which is so common in Scripture to sexual immorality or to spiritual infidelity?

(i) There is no doubt that in Scripture infidelity to God is expressed in terms of fornication and adultery. Israel is the Bride of God (*Isaiah* 54: 5; *Jeremiah* 3: 20); and in the New Testament the Church is the Bride of Christ (2 *Corinthians* 11: 1, 2; *Ephesians* 5: 24–28). Again and again in the Old Testament the Israelites are, therefore, said to "play the harlot after strange gods" (*Exodus* 34: 15, 16; *Deuteronomy* 31: 16; *Hosea* 9: 1). In the New Testament the age which is unfaithful to Jesus Christ is an "evil and adulterous generation" (*Matthew* 12: 39; 16: 4; *Mark* 8: 38). Is the *fornication* which Jezebel's teaching inculcated a spiritual infidelity to Jesus Christ? If that is the meaning, her *paramours* (verse 22) will be those who are flirting with this kind of teaching and her *children* (verse 23) those who have accepted it.

It may well be that the teaching of Jezebel was that the Christians did not need to be so exclusive in their worship of Jesus Christ and, above all, that there was no need for them to refuse to say, "Caesar is Lord," and to burn their pinch of incense. If the Christian Church as a whole had accepted that form of teaching, the inevitable consequence would have been that Christianity would have become nothing more than still another of those religions of which the Roman Empire was so full. The claim of Christianity is not that Jesus Christ is one of the Saviours nor even the chief of Saviours; but that he is the only Saviour.

(ii) One thing in the letter militates against that view. We read that the followers of Jezebel claimed to know *the depths of Satan* (verse 24). Some scholars think that this is the Risen Christ's contemptuous description of the false teaching. The real Christian knows what Paul called the deep things of God (1 *Corinthians* 2: 10); what Jezebel and her company know is the deep things of Satan. But that will not do, for the letter unmistakably speaks of "the deep things of Satan, as

they call them." This is quite certainly a reference to a kind
of belief that was not uncommom among the heretics. Some
of them held that it was a plain duty to experience every
kind of sin. The real achievement was to allow the body to
wallow in sin and to keep the soul unaffected. Those who
knew the deep things of Satan were those who had deliberately plumbed evil to its depths. Jezebel may well have been
teaching that it was a duty to sin.

It seems to us that in this case all the threads tie up and
there is no necessity to make a choice between views. All the
probability is that Jezebel was teaching that a Christian ought
to accommodate himself to the world; in other words she
was urging on the Church a spiritual infidelity which was
bound to issue in physical fornication. It is in the mercy of
God that the teaching of Jezebel and her like did not become
the view of the Church. If that had happened, the Church
would have become a kind of pleasant paganism. On this
Paul said: "Do not be conformed to this world, but be trans-
formed by the renewal of your mind" (*Romans* 12: 2). And
Jesus said the last word on the matter: "No one can serve
two masters. . . . You cannot serve God and mammon" (*Matthew* 6: 24). The old choice is still the new choice: "Choose
you this day whom you will serve" (*Deuteronomy* 30: 19;
Joshua 24: 15).

THYATIRA
PROMISES AND THREATS

Revelation 2: 18–29 (*continued*)

(4) THE letter to Thyatira finishes with a series of great threats
and great promises. Jezebel has been given all the latitude the
divine mercy can give her. If she does not repent, she will
be cast into a bed of sickness and her paramours and followers
will share her fate. This will prove to all men that indeed the
Risen Christ, as the Authorized Version has it, "searches the
reins and hearts." The phrase is a translation of *Jeremiah*
11: 20. In *Jeremiah* the prerogative of searching the inmost

thoughts of men belongs to God; but in the *Revelation*, as so often, the prerogatives of God have become the prerogatives of the Risen Christ.

The *reins* are the *kidneys*; strange as it may seem to us, Hebrew psychology believed that the seat of emotion was in the lower viscera, the kidneys and the bowels; and the seat of thought was in the heart. When the Risen Christ says that he will search the reins and the heart, it means that every emotion and every thought will be open to his gaze.

There is real point here. When we began to study the letter to Thyatira we saw that anyone coming into that Church for the first time would have believed it to be surging with life and fruitful in every good work. No doubt those who prospered in business because of their compromise with the world were lavish in their liberality. No doubt those who attended the trade guilds gave generously to charitable funds. They *looked* like real Christians. No doubt Jezebel seemed to many a fine character. She must have had a command of language and a fine presence to be regarded as a prophetess. The point here is that the Risen Christ can see beyond the outward disguise; he will know whether or not her repentance is real.

To those who are faithful the promise is made and it is twofold.

(i) The first part comes from *Psalm* 2: 8, 9; "Ask of me and I will make the nations your heritage, and the ends of the earth your possession. You shall break them with a rod of iron, and dash them in pieces like a potter's vessel." In Jewish belief that was a Messianic Psalm, thinking of a conquering Messiah who would smash the heathen and extend the rule of Israel to the ends of the earth. But it has also been one of the great missionary inspirations of the Christian Church. Many a missionary claimed that promise: "Ask of me, and I will make the nations your heritage."

(ii) The second part is the promise of the morning star. Four main interpretations have been given.

(*a*) It is taken as a promise of the first resurrection. As the morning star rises after the night, so the Christian will rise after the night of death.

(*b*) It is taken as the conquest of Lucifer. Lucifer is the devil, the angel who was so proud that he rebelled against God and was cast over the battlements of heaven (*Isaiah* 14: 12). *Lucifer* means *light-bringer* and it is the name of the morning star. If that be so, this is a promise of complete power over Satan and over sin.

(iii) This has been referred to *Daniel* 12: 3. There the promise is: "and those who are wise shall shine like the brightness of the firmament; and those who turn many to righteousness like the stars for ever and ever." If that be so, the morning star is the glory which will come to those who are righteous and have helped others to walk in the paths of righteousness.

(iv) All these are very lovely and may all be involved in this promise; but we are quite certain that the correct interpretation is this. The *Revelation* itself calls Jesus "the bright morning star" (*Revelation* 22: 16). The promise of the morning star is the promise of Christ himself. If the Christian is true, when life comes to an end he will possess Christ, never to lose him any more.

THE LETTER TO SARDIS

Revelation 3: 1–6

And to the angel of the Church in Sardis, write:

These things says he who has the seven Spirits of God and the seven stars.

I know your works; I know that you have a reputation for life, but that you are dead. Show yourself watchful, and strengthen what remains and what is going to die. I have not found your works completed before my God. Remember, then, how you received and heard the gospel, and keep it, and repent. If, then, you are not on the watch, I will come as a thief, and you will not know at what hour I will come to you.

But you have a few people in Sardis who have not defiled their garments and they will walk with me in white raiment, because they are worthy. He who overcomes will be thus clothed in white raiment and I will not wipe his name out of the Book of Life, but I will acknowledge his name before my Father and before his angels.

Let him who has an ear hear what the Spirit is saying to the Churches.

SARDIS
PAST SPLENDOUR AND PRESENT DECAY

Revelation 3: 1–6

SIR W. M. RAMSAY said of Sardis that nowhere was there a greater example of the melancholy contrast between past splendour and present decay. Sardis was a city of degeneration.

Seven hundred years before this letter was written Sardis had been one of the greatest cities in the world. There the king of Lydia ruled over his empire in oriental splendour. At that time Sardis was a city of the east and was hostile to the Greek world, Aeschylus wrote of it: "They that dwelt by Tmolous pledged themselves to cast the yoke on Hellas."

Sardis stood in the midst of the plain of the valley of the River Hermus. To the north of that plain rose the long ridge of Mount Tmolus; from that ridge a series of hills went out like spurs, each forming a narrow plateau. On one of these spurs, fifteen hundred feet up, stood the original Sardis. Clearly such a position made it almost impregnable. The sides of the ridge were smoothly precipitous; and only where the spur met the ridge of Mount Tmolus was there any possible approach into Sardis and even that was hard and steep. It has been said that Sardis stood like some gigantic watch-tower guarding the Hermus valley. The time came when the narrow space on the top of the plateau was too small for the expanding city; and Sardis grew round the foot of the spur on which the citadel stood. The name Sardis (*Sardeis* in Greek) is really a plural noun, for there were two towns, one on the plateau and one in the valley beneath.

The wealth of Sardis was legendary. Through the lower town flowed the River Pactolus, which was said in the old days to have had gold-bearing waters from which much of the wealth of Sardis came. Greatest of the Sardian kings was Croesus, whose name is still commemorated in the proverb, "As rich as Croesus." It was with him that Sardis reached its zenith and it was with him that it plunged to disaster.

It was not that Croesus was not warned where Sardis was heading. Solon, the wisest of the Greeks, came on a visit and was shown the magnificence and the luxury. He saw the blind confidence of Croesus and his people that nothing could end this splendour; but he also saw that the seeds of softness and of degeneration were being sown. And it was then that he uttered his famous saying to Croesus: "Call no man happy until he is dead." Solon knew only too well the chances and changes of life which Croesus had forgotten.

Croesus embarked upon a war with Cyrus of Persia which was the end of the greatness of Sardis. Again Croesus was warned, but he failed to see the warning. To get at the armies of Cyrus he had to cross the River Halys. He took counsel of the famous oracle at Delphi and was told: "If you cross the River Halys, you will destroy a great empire." Croesus took it as a promise that he would annihilate the Persians; it never crossed his mind that it was a prophecy that the campaign on which he had embarked would be the end of his own power.

He crossed the Halys, engaged in battle and was routed. He was not in the least worried, for he thought that all he had to do as to retire to the impregnable citadel of Sardis, recuperate and fight again. Cyrus initiated the siege of Sardis, waited for fourteen days, then offered a special reward to anyone who would find an entry into the city.

The rock on which Sardis was built was friable, more like close packed dried mud than rock. The nature of the rock meant that it developed cracks. A certain Mardian soldier called Hyeroeades had seen a Sardian soldier accidentally drop his helmet over the battlements, and then make his way down the precipice to retrieve it. Hyeroeades knew that there must be a crack in the rock there by means of which an agile man could climb up. That night he led a party of Persian troops up by the fault in the rock. When they reached the top they found the battlements completely unguarded.

The Sardians had thought themselves too safe to need a

guard; and so Sardis fell. A city with a history like that knew what the Risen Christ was talking about when he said: "Watch!"

There were a few futile attempts at rebellion; but Cyrus followed a deliberate policy. He forbade any Sardian to possess a weapon of war. He ordered them to wear tunics and buskins, that is, actor's boots, instead of sandals. He ordered them to teach their sons lyre-playing, the song and the dance, and retail trading. Sardis had been flabby already but the last vestige of spirit was banished from its people and it became a city of degeneration.

It vanished from history under Persian rule for two centuries. In due time it surrendered to Alexander the Great and through him it became a city of Greek culture. Then history repeated itself. After the death of Alexander there were many claimants for the power. Antiochus, who became the ruler of the area in which Sardis stood, was at war with a rival called Achaeus who sought refuge in Sardis. For a year Antiochus besieged him; then a soldier called Lagoras repeated the exploit of Hyeroeades. At night with a band of brave men he climbed the steep cliffs. The Sardians had forgotten their lesson. There was no guard and once again Sardis fell because it was not upon the watch.

In due times the Romans came. Sardis was still a wealthy city. It was a centre of the woollen trade; and it was claimed that the art of dyeing wool was actually discovered there. It became a Roman assize town. In A.D. 17 it was destroyed by an earthquake which devasted the area. Tiberius, the Roman Emperor, in his kindness remitted all tribute for five years and gave a donation of 10,000,000 sesterces, that is, £400,000. towards rebuilding and Sardis recovered itself by the easy way.

When John wrote his letter to Sardis, it was wealthy but degenerate. Even the once great citadel was now only an ancient monument on the hill top. There was no life or spirit there. The once great Sardians were soft, and twice they had lost their city because they were too lazy to watch. In

that enervating atmosphere the Christian Church too had lost
its vitality and was a corpse instead of a living Church.

SARDIS
DEATH IN LIFE

Revelation 3: 1–6 (*continued*)

IN the introduction to this letter the Risen Christ is described in two phrases.

(i) He is he who has the seven Spirits of God. We have
already come upon this strange phrase in *Revelation* 1: 4. It
has two aspects of meaning. (*a*) It denotes the Holy Spirit
with his sevenfold gifts, an idea founded on the description
of the Spirit in *Isaiah* 11: 2. (*b*) It denotes the Spirit in his
sevenfold operation. There are seven Churches, yet in each
of them the Spirit operates with all his presence and power.
The *seven spirits* signifies the completeness of the gifts of the
Spirit and the universality of his presence.

(ii) He is he who has the seven stars. The stars stand for
the Churches and their angels. The Church is the possession
of Jesus Christ. Many a time men act as if the Church
belonged to them, but it belongs to Jesus Christ and all in
it are his servants. In any decision regarding the Church,
the decisive factor must be not what any man wishes the
Church to do but what Jesus Christ wishes to be done.

The terrible accusation against the Church at Sardis is that,
although it has a reputation for life, it is, in fact, spiritually
dead. The New Testament frequently likens sin to death. In the
Pastoral Epistles we read: "She who is self-indulgent is dead
even while she lives" (1 *Timothy* 5: 6), The Prodigal Son
is he who was dead and is alive again (*Luke* 15: 24). The
Roman Christians are men who have been brought from
death to life (*Romans* 6: 13). Paul says that his converts in
their pre-Christian days were dead through trespasses and sins
(*Ephesians* 2: 1, 5).

(i) Sin is the *death of the will*. If a man accepts the
invitations of sin for long enough, the time comes when he

cannot accept anything else. Habits grow upon him until he can no longer break them. A man comes, as Seneca had it, to hate his sins and to love them at the same time. There can be few of us who have not experienced the power of some habit into which we have fallen.

(ii) Sin is the *death of the feelings*. The process of becoming the slave of sin does not happen overnight. The first time a man sins he does so with many a qualm. But the day comes, if he goes on taking what is forbidden, when he does without a qualm that which once he would have been horrified to do. Sin, as Burns had it, "petrifies the feeling."

(iii) Sin is the *death of all loveliness*. The terrible thing about sin is that it can take the loveliest things and turn them into ugliness. Through sin the yearning for the highest can become the craving for power; the wish to serve can become the intoxication of ambition; the desire of love can become the passion of lust. Sin is the killer of life's loveliness.

It is only by the grace of God that we can escape the death of sin.

SARDIS
A LIFELESS CHURCH

Revelation 3: 1–6 (*continued*)

THE lifelessness of the Church at Sardis had a strange effect.

(i) The Church at Sardis was untroubled by any heresy. Heresy is always the product of the searching mind; it is, in fact, the sign of a Church that is alive. There is nothing worse than a state in which a man is orthodox because he is too lazy to think for himself. He is actually better with a heresy which he holds intensely than with an orthodoxy about which in his heart of hearts he does not care.

(ii) The Church at Sardis was untroubled by any attack from the outside, neither by the heathen or by the Jews. The truth was that it was so lifeless that it was not worth attacking. The Pastoral Epistles describe those who had drifted away from the true faith by saying that they had a form of godliness but denied its power (2 *Timothy* 3: 5). Moffatt translates it: "Though they keep up a form of religion, they will have nothing to do with it as a force." Phillips puts it: "They will maintain a façade of 'religion,' but their conduct will deny its validity."

A truly vital Church will always be under attack. "Woe to you," said Jesus, "when all men speak well of you!" (*Luke* 6: 26). A Church with a positive message is bound to be one to which there will be opposition.

A Church which is so lethargic as to fail to produce a heresy is mentally dead; and a Church which is so negative as to fail to produce opposition is dead in its witness to Christ.

SARDIS
WATCH!

Revelation 3: 1–6 (*continued*)

IF anything is to be rescued from the impending ruin of the Church in Sardis the Christians there must wake from their deadly lethargy and watch. No commandment appears more frequently in the New Testament than that to watch.

(i) Watchfulness should be the constant attitude of the Christian life. "It is full time," says Paul, "to wake from sleep" (*Romans* 13: 11). "Be watchful, stand firm in your faith," he urges (1 *Corinthians* 16: 13). It has been said that "eternal vigilance is the price of liberty" and eternal watchfulness is the price of salvation.

(ii) The Christian must be on the watch against the wiles of the devil (1 *Peter* 5: 8). The history of Sardis had its vivid examples of what happens to the garrison whose watch is slack. The Christian is under continual attack by the powers which seek to seduce him from his loyalty to Christ. Often these attacks are subtle. He must, therefore, be ever on the watch.

(iii) The Christian must be on the watch against temptation. "Watch and pray," said Jesus, "that you may not enter into temptation" (*Matthew* 26: 41). Temptation waits for our unguarded moments and then attacks. In the Christian life there must be unceasing vigilance against it.

(iv) Repeatedly the New Testament urges the Christian to be on the watch for the coming of his Lord. "Watch, therefore," said Jesus, "for you do not know on what day your Lord is coming." "What I say to you, I say to all: watch" (*Matthew* 24: 42, 43; *Mark* 13: 37). "Let us not sleep, as others do," writes Paul to the Thessalonians. "Let us keep awake and be sober" (1 *Thessalonians* 5: 6). No man knows the day and the hour when for him eternity will invade time. "The last day is a secret," says Augustine, "that every day may be watched." A man should live every day as if it were his last.

(v) The Christian must be on the watch against false teaching. In Paul's last address to the elders of Ephesus he warns them that grievous wolves will invade the flock from outside and from inside men will arise to speak perverse things. "Therefore," he says, "watch!" (*Acts* 20: 29–31).

(vi) Nor must the Christian forget that, even as he must watch for Jesus Christ, Jesus Christ is watching him. "I have not found your works perfect," says the Risen Christ, "in the sight of my God." Here two great truths meet us. (*a*) Christ is looking for something from us. We so often regard him as the one to whom we look for things; for his strength, his help, his support, his comfort. But we must never forget that he is looking for our love, our loyalty and our service. (*b*) The things a man must do lie to his hand. The old saying is true: "Fate is what we must do; destiny is what we are meant to do." The Christian does not believe in an inescapable fate; but he does believe in a destiny which he can accept or refuse.

From everyone of us Jesus Christ is looking for something; and for everyone of us there is something to do.

SARDIS
THE IMPERATIVES OF THE RISEN LORD

Revelation 3: 1–6 (*continued*)

In verse 3 we have a series of imperatives.

(i) The Risen Christ says: "*Remember* how you received and heard the gospel." It is the present imperative and means: "Keep on remembering; never allow yourself to forget." The Risen Christ is telling the lethargic Sardians to remember the thrill with which they first heard the good news. It is a fact of life that certain things sharpen memory which has grown dull. When, for instance, we return to a graveside, the sorrow from which the years have taken the edge grows piercingly poignant again. Ever and again the Christian must stand before the Cross and remember again what God has done for him.

(ii) The Risen Christ says: "*Repent!*" This is an aorist imperative and describes one definite action. In the Christian life there must be a decisive moment, when a man decides to be done with the old way and to begin on the new.

(iii) The Risen Christ says: "*Keep* the commands of the gospel." Here again we have a present imperative indicating continuous action. It means: "Never stop keeping the commands of the gospel." Here is a warning against what we might call "spasmodic Christianity." Too many of us are Christian one moment and unchristian the next.

(iv) There is the command *to watch*. There is an old Latin saying that "the gods walk on feet that are wrapped in wool." Their approach is silent and unobserved, until a man finds himself without warning facing eternity. But that cannot happen if every day a man lives in the presence of Christ; he who walks hand-in-hand with Christ cannot be taken unawares by his coming.

SARDIS
THE FAITHFUL FEW

Revelation 3: 1–6 (*continued*)

IN verse 4 there shines through the darkness a ray of hope. Even in Sardis there are the faithful few. When Abraham is pleading with God for Sodom, he appeals to God: "To slay the righteous with the wicked, far be that from thee" (*Genesis* 18: 25). In the old story of the kings, Abijah alone of all the sons of Jeroboam was spared because in him was found some good thing toward the Lord God of Israel (1 *Kings* 14: 13). God never abandons his search for the faithful few and they are never lost to his sight in the mass of the wicked.

It is said of the faithful that they "have not soiled their garments." James spoke with respect and admiration of the man who kept himself "unstained from the world" (*James* 1: 27). There are two possible pictures here.

(i) In the heathen world no worshipper was allowed to approach a temple of the gods with soiled clothes. For the heathen this was an external thing; but this may describe the man who has kept his soul clean so that he can enter into the presence of God and not be ashamed.

(ii) Swete thinks that the white garments stand for the profession a man made at baptism; and that the phrase described the man who had not broken his baptismal vows. At this stage in the Church's history baptism was adult baptism, and at baptism a man took his personal pledge to Jesus Christ. This is all the more likely because it was common at baptism to clothe a man, after he had emerged from the water, in clean white robes, symbolic of the cleansing of his life. The man who is faithful to his pledge will, beyond a doubt, some day hear God say: "Well done!"

To those who have been true the promise is that they will walk with God. Again there is a double background.

(*a*) There may be a heathen background. At the Persian court the king's most trusted favourites were given the privilege of walking in the royal gardens with the king and were called "The Companions of the Garden." Those who have been true to God will some day walk with him in Paradise.

(*b*) There may be a reference to the old story of Enoch. "And Enoch walked with God, and he was not; for God took him" (*Genesis* 5: 24). Enoch walked with God on earth and continued to walk with him in the heavenly places. The man whose walk with God is close on earth will enter into a nearer companionship with him when the end of life comes.

SARDIS
THE THREEFOLD PROMISE

Revelation 3: 1-6 (*continued*)

To those who have been faithful comes the threefold promise.

(i) They will be clothed with white raiment. It is said of the righteous that "they will shine forth like the sun in the Kingdom of their Father" (*Matthew* 13: 43); and it is said of God that he covers himself with light as with a garment (*Psalm* 104: 2). What do the white robes signify?

(*a*) In the ancient world white robes stood for *festivity*. "Let your garments be always white," said the preacher, "and let not oil be lacking on your head" (*Ecclesiastes* 9: 8). The white robes may stand for the fact that the faithful will be guests at the banquet of God.

(*b*) In the ancient world white robes stood for *victory*. On the day when a Roman triumph was celebrated, all the citizens clad themselves in white; the city itself was called *urbs candida*, the city in white. The white robes may stand for the reward of those who have won the victory.

(*c*) In any land and time white is the colour of *purity*, and the white robes may stand for the purity whose reward is to see God. "Blessed are the pure in heart, for they shall see God" (*Matthew* 5: 8).

(*d*) It has been suggested that the white robes stand for

the resurrection bodies which the faithful will some day wear. They who are faithful will share in that whiteness of light which is the garment of God himself.

We need not make a choice between these various meanings; we may well believe that they are all included in the greatness of the promise.

(ii) Their names will not be wiped out of the Book of Life. The Book of Life is a conception which occurs often in the Bible. Moses is willing to be wiped out of the book which God has written, if by his sacrifice he can save his people from the consequence of their sin (*Exodus* 32: 32, 33). It is the hope of the Psalmist that the wicked will be blotted out of the book of the living (*Psalm* 69: 28). In the time of judgment those who are written in the book will be delivered (*Daniel* 12: 1). The names of Paul's fellow-labourers for God are written in the book of life (*Philippians* 4: 3). He who is not written in the book of life is cast into the lake of fire (*Revelation* 20: 15); only they who are written in the Lamb's book of life shall enter into blessedness (*Revelation* 21: 27).

In the ancient world a king kept a register of his citizens. When a man committed a crime against the state, or when he died, his name was erased from that register. To have one's name written in the book of life is to be numbered amongst the faithful citizens of the Kingdom of God.

(iii) Jesus Christ will confess their names before his Father and the angels. It was Jesus's promise that, if a man confessed him before men, he would confess him before his Father; and if a man denied him before men, he would deny him before his Father (*Matthew* 10: 32, 33; *Luke* 12: 8, 9). Jesus Christ is for ever true to the man who is true to him.

THE LETTER TO PHILADELPHIA

Revelation 3: 7–13

And to the angel of the Church in Philadelphia, write:

These things says he who is holy, he who is true, he who has the key of David, he who opens and no man will shut, and shuts and no man opens. I know your works. Behold, I have set before you a door which stands open and which no man shuts, because you have a little strength and because you have kept my word, and have not denied my name. Behold, I will give you those who belong to the synagogue of Satan, who call themselves Jews and who are not, but who lie. Behold, I will make them come and kneel before your feet, and they will know that I have loved you. Because you have kept my command to endure, I, too, will keep you safe from the hour of testing, which is to come upon the whole inhabited world, to test those who dwell upon the earth. I am coming quickly. Hold on to what you have, that no one may take your crown.

I will make him who overcomes a pillar in the temple of my God and he will go out no more; and I will write upon him the name of my God, and the name of the city of my God, of the new Jerusalem, which is coming down from heaven from my God, and my new name.

Let him who has an ear hear what the Spirit is saying to the Churches.

PHILADELPHIA
CITY OF PRAISE

Revelation 3: 7–13

PHILADELPHIA was the youngest of all the seven cities. It was founded by colonists from Pergamum under the reign of Attalus the Second, who ruled in Pergamum from 159 to 138 B.C. *Philadelphos* is the Greek for *one who loves his brother*. Such was the love of Attalus for his brother Eumenes that he was called Philadelphos, and it was after him that Philadelphia was named.

It was founded for a special purpose. It was situated where the borders of Mysia, Lydia and Phrygia met. But it was not as a garrison town that Philadelphia was founded, for there was little danger there. It was founded with the deliberate intention that it might be a missionary of Greek culture and language to Lydia and Phrygia; and so well did it do its work that by A.D. 19 the Lydians had forgotten their own language and were all but Greeks. Ramsay says of Philadelphia that it was "the centre for the diffusion of Greek language and Greek letters in a peaceful land and by peaceful means." That is what the Risen Christ means when he speaks of the open door that is set before Philadelphia. Three centuries before, Philadelphia had been given an open door to spread Greek ideas in the lands beyond; and now there has come to it another great missionary opportunity, to carry to men who never knew it the message of the love of Jesus Christ.

Philadelphia had a great characteristic which has left its mark upon this letter. It was on the edge of a great plain called the *Katakekaumenē,* which means the Burned Land. The *Katakekaumenē* was a great volcanic plain bearing the marks of the lava and the ashes of volcanoes then extinct. Such land is fertile; and Philadelphia was the centre of a great grape-growing area and a famous producer of wines. But that situation had its perils, and these perils had left their mark more deeply on Philadelphia than on any other city. In A.D. 17 there came a great earthquake which destroyed Sardis and ten other cities. In Philadelphia the tremors went on for years; Strabo describes it as a "city full of earthquakes."

It often happens that, when a great earthquake comes, people meet it with courage and self-possession, but ever-recurring minor shocks drive them to sheer panic. That is what happened in Philadelphia. Strabo describes the scene. Shocks were an everyday occurrence. Gaping cracks appeared in the walls of the houses. Now one part of the city was in ruins, now another. Most of the population lived outside the city in huts and feared even to go on the city streets lest they should be killed by falling masonry. Those who still dared to live in the city were reckoned mad; they spent their time shoring up the shaking buildings and every now and then fleeing to the open spaces for safety. These terrible days in Philadelphia were never wholly forgotten, and people in it ever waited subconsciously for the ominous tremors of the ground, ready to flee for their lives to the open spaces. People in Philadelphia well knew what security lay in a promise that "they would go out no more."

But there is more of Philadelphia's history than that in this letter. When this earthquake devastated it, Tiberius was as generous to Philadelphia as he had been to Sardis. In gratitude it changed its name to Neocaesarea—the New City of Caesar. In the time of Vespasian Philadelphia was in gratitude to change its name again to Flavia, for Flavius was the Emperor's family name. It is true that neither of these new names lasted and "Philadelphia" was restored. But the people of Philadelphia well knew what it was to receive "a new name."

Of all the cities Philadelphia receives the greatest praise and it was to show that it deserved it.

In later days it became a very great city. When the Turks and Mohammedanism flooded across Asia Minor and every other town had fallen, Philadelphia stood erect. For centuries it was a free Greek Christian city amidst a pagan people. It was the last bastion of Asian Christianity. It was not till midway through the fourteenth century that it fell; and to this day there is a Christian bishop and a thousand Christians in it. With the exception of Smyrna the other Churches are in ruins but Philadelphia still holds aloft the banner of the Christian faith.

PHILADELPHIA
TITLES AND CLAIMS

Revelation 3: 7–13 (*continued*)

In the introduction to this letter the Risen Christ is called by three great titles, each of which implies a tremendous claim.

(i) He is he who is holy. Holy is the description of God himself. "Holy, holy, holy is the Lord of hosts," was the song of the seraphs which Isaiah heard (*Isaiah* 6: 3). "To whom then will you compare me, that I should be like him? says the Holy One" (*Isaiah* 40: 25). "I am the Lord, your Holy One, the creator of Israel, your King" (*Isaiah* 43: 15). All through the Old Testament God is the Holy One; and now that title is given to the Risen Christ. We must remember that *holy* (*hagios*) means *different, separate from*. God is holy because he is different from men; he has that quality of being which belongs to him alone. To say that Jesus Christ is holy is to say that he shares the being of God.

(ii) He is he who is true. In Greek there are two words for *true*. There is *alēthēs*, which means *true* in the sense that a true statement is different from a false statement. There is *alēthinos*, which means *real* as opposed to that which is unreal. It is the second of these words which is used here. In Jesus is reality. When we are confronted with him, we are confronted with no shadowy outline of the truth but with the truth itself.

(iii) He is he who has the key of David, who opens and no man will shut, who shuts and no man opens. We may first note that the key is *the symbol of authority*. Here is the picture of

Jesus Christ as the one who has the final authority which no one can question.

Behind this there is an Old Testament picture. Hezekiah had a faithful steward called Eliakim, who was over all his house and who alone could admit to the presence of the king. Isaiah heard God say of this faithful Eliakim: "and I will place on his shoulder the key of the house of David; he shall open, and none shall shut; and he shall shut, and none shall open" (*Isaiah* 22: 22). It is this picture which is in John's mind. Jesus alone has authority to admit to the new Jerusalem, the new city of David. As the *Te Deum* has it: "Thou didst open the kingdom of Heaven to all believers." He is the new and living way into the presence of God.

PHILADELPHIA
THE OPEN DOOR

Revelation 3: 7–13 (*continued*)

IN verses 8 and 9 there is a problem of punctuation. In the early Greek manuscripts there was no punctuation at all. The problem is that the words "because you have a little strength, and because you have kept my word, and have not denied my name," can go equally well with what precedes them or with what follows. They may express either the reason why the door stands open before the Christians of Philadelphia or the reason why they will be given those who belong to the synagogue of Satan. We have taken them with the words which precede them.

It is the great promise of the Risen Christ that he has set before the Christians of Philadelphia an open door which no man can ever shut. What is the meaning of this open door?

(i) It may be the door of missionary opportunity. Writing to the Corinthians of the work which lies ahead of him, Paul says: "For a wide door for effective work has opened to me"

(1 *Corinthians* 16: 9). When he came to Troas, a door was opened to him by the Lord (2 *Corinthians* 2: 12). He asks the Colossians to pray that a door of utterance may be opened for him (*Colossians* 4: 3). When he came back to Antioch he told how God had opened the door of faith to the Gentiles (*Acts* 14: 27).

This meaning is particularly appropriate for Philadelphia. We have seen how it was a border town, standing where the boundaries of Lydia, Mysia and Phrygia met, and founded to be a missionary of Greek language and culture to the barbarous peoples beyond. It was on the road of the imperial postal service, which left the coast at Troas, came to Philadelphia *via* Pergamum, Thyatira and Sardis, and joined the great road out to Phrygia. The armies of Caesar travelled that road; the caravans of the merchant-men travelled it; and now it was beckoning the missionaries of Christ.

Two things emerge here. (*a*) There is a door of missionary opportunity before every man and he need not go overseas to find it. Within the home, within the circle in which we move, within the parish in which we reside, there are those to be won for Christ. To use that door of opportunity is at once our privilege and our responsibility. (*b*) In the way of Christ the reward of work well done is more work to do. Philadelphia had proved faithful and the reward for her fidelity was still more work to do for Christ.

(ii) It has been suggested that the door which is set before the Philadelphians is none other than Jesus himself. "I am the door," said Jesus (*John* 10: 7, 9).

(iii) It has been suggested that the door is the door to the Messianic community. With Jesus Christ the new kingdom of David was inaugurated; and, just as in the ancient kingdom Eliakim had the keys to admit to the royal presence, so Jesus is the door to admit to the kingdom of God.

(iv) Apart from all these things, for any man the door of prayer is always open. That is a door which no man can ever shut and it is one which Jesus opened when he assured men of the seeking love of God the Father.

PHILADELPHIA
INHERITORS OF THE PROMISE

Revelation 3: 7–13 (*continued*)

IN verse 9 the promise of the Risen Christ is that some day the Jews who slander the Christians will kneel before them. This is an echo of an expectation of the Jews which finds frequent expression in the Old Testament.

This was that in the new age, all nations would do humble homage to the Jews. This promise recurs again and again in *Isaiah*. "The sons of those who oppressed you shall come bending low to you; and all who despised you shall bow down at your feet" (*Isaiah* 60: 14). "The wealth of Egypt and the merchandise of Ethiopia and the Sabeans, men of stature, shall come over to you and be yours, they shall follow you; they shall come over in chains and bow down to you" (*Isaiah* 45: 14). "Kings shall be your foster fathers, and their queens your nursing mothers; with their faces to the ground they shall bow down to you, and lick the dust of your feet" (*Isaiah* 49: 23). Zechariah has a vision of the day when all men of all nations and languages shall turn to Jerusalem, "they shall take hold of the robe of a Jew, saying, 'Let us go with you, for we have heard that God is with you'" (*Zechariah* 8: 22, 23).

It was the Christian belief that the Jewish nation had lost its place in the plan of God and that that place had passed to the Church. A Jew in God's sense of the term was not one who could claim racial descent from Abraham but one of any nation who had made the same venture of faith as he had (*Romans* 9: 6–9). The Church was the Israel of God (*Galatians* 6: 16). It was, therefore, now true that all the promises which had been made to Israel had been inherited by the Church. It was to her that one day all men would humbly make their submission. This promise is a reversal of all that the Jews had expected; they had expected that all nations would kneel before them; but the day was to come when they with all nations would kneel before Christ.

That is what the Philadelphian Church would see, at least in its beginnings, if its members were faithful. Up until now they had been faithful. In the sentence, "You have kept my word, and have not denied my name," both the verbs are in the aorist tense, which describes one definite act in past time; and the implication is that there had been some time of trial out of which the Philadelphian Church had emerged triumphantly true. They may have only a little strength; their resources may be small; but, if they are faithful, they will see the dawn of the triumph of Christ.

> Though few and small and weak your bands,
>   Strong in your Captain's strength,
> Go to the conquest of all lands;
>   All must be his at length.

That which must keep a Christian faithful is the vision of a world for Christ, for the coming of such a world depends on the fidelity of the individual Christian.

PHILADELPHIA
THOSE WHO KEEP ARE KEPT

Revelation 3: 7–13 (*continued*)

IT is the promise of the Risen Christ that he who keeps will be kept. "You have kept my commandment," he says, "therefore, I will keep you." Loyalty has its sure reward. In verse 10 in the Greek the phrase *my command to endure* is highly concentrated. Literally, it is *the word of my endurance*. The real meaning is that the promise is to those who have practised the same kind of endurance as Jesus displayed in his earthly life.

When we are called upon to show endurance, the endurance of Jesus Christ supplies us with three things. First, it supplies us with an example. Second, it supplies us with an inspiration. We must walk looking to him, who for the joy that was set before him endured the cross despising the shame (*Hebrews* 12: 1, 2). Third, the endurance of Jesus Christ is the guarantee of his sympathy with us when we are called upon to endure. "Because he himself has suffered and been tempted, he is able to help those who are tempted" (*Hebrews* 2: 18).

In verse 10 we are back again amidst beliefs which are characteristically Jewish. As we have so often seen, the Jews divided time into two ages, the present age which is wholly bad, and the age to come, which is wholly good with in between the terrible time of destruction when judgment will fall upon the world. It is to that terrible time that John refers. Even when times comes to an end, and the world as we know it ceases to exist, he who is faithful to Christ will still be safe in his keeping.

PHILADELPHIA
PROMISE AND WARNING

Revelation 3: 7–13 (*continued*)

IN verse 11 there is promise and warning combined.

The Risen Christ tells them that he is coming quickly. It has been said that in the New Testament the Coming of Christ is continually used for two purposes.

(i) It is used as *a warning to the heedless*. Jesus himself tells of the wicked servant, who took advantage of his master's absence to conduct himself evilly and to whom the master made a sudden return that brought judgment. (*Matthew* 24: 48–51). Paul warns the Thessalonians of the terrible fate which awaits the disobedient and the unbelieving when the Lord Jesus shall be revealed from heaven and shall take swift and final vengeance on his enemies (2 *Thessalonians* 1: 7–9). Peter warns his people that they will give account for their deeds to him who comes to judge the living and the dead (1 *Peter* 4: 5).

(ii) It is used as a *comfort to the oppressed.* James urges patient endurance on his people because the coming of the Lord is drawing near (*James* 5: 8); soon their distresses will be at an end. The writer to the Hebrews urges patience, for soon he that shall come will come (*Hebrews* 10: 37).

In the New Testament men used the idea of the Coming of Christ as a warning to the heedless and as a comfort to the oppressed. It is quite true that, in the literal sense, Jesus Christ did not come back to those who were so warned and exhorted. But no man knows when eternity will invade his life and God will bid him rise and come; and that must warn the careless to prepare to meet his God and cheer the oppressed with the thought of the coming glory of the faithful soul.

There is another warning here. The Risen Christ bids the Philadelphians hold to what they have, that no one may take their crown (verse 11). It is not a question of someone stealing their crown but of God taking it from them and giving it to someone else, because they were not worthy to wear it. Trench makes a list of people in the Bible who lost their place to someone else because they had shown that they were not fit to hold it. Esau lost his place to Jacob (*Genesis* 25: 34; 27: 36). Reuben, unstable as water, lost his place to Judah (*Genesis* 49: 4, 8). Saul lost his place to David (1 *Samuel* 16: 1, 13). Shebna lost his place to Eliakim (*Isaiah* 22: 15–25). Joab and Abiathar lost their places to Benaiah and Zadok (1 *Kings* 2: 25). Judas lost his place to Matthias (*Acts* 1: 25, 26). The Jews lost their place to the Gentiles (*Romans* 11: 11).

There is tragedy here. It sometimes happens that a man is given a task to do and goes towards it with the highest hopes; but it begins to be seen that he is too small for the task and he is removed from the task and it is given to someone else. That can happen with the tasks of God. God has a task for every man; but it may be that the man proves himself unfit for the task and it is given to another.

It is blessedly true that even out of failure a man can redeem himself—but only if he casts himself upon the grace of Jesus Christ.

PHILADELPHIA
MANY PROMISES

Revelation 3: 7–13 (*continued*)

IN verse 12 we come to the promises of the Risen Christ to those who are faithful. They are many and most would paint pictures which would be vivid and real to the people of Philadelphia.

(i) The faithful Christian will be a pillar in the Temple of God. A pillar of the Church is a great and honoured support. Peter and James and John were the pillars of the early church in Jerusalem (*Galatians* 2: 9). Abraham, said the Jewish Rabbis, was the pillar of the world.

(ii) The faithful Christian will go out no more. There may be something of two meanings here.

(*a*) This may be a promise of security. We have seen how for years Philadelphia was terrorized by recurring earthquakes of the earth and how, when such times came, its citizens fled into the open country to escape and, when the tremors ended, came uncertainly back. Life was lived in an atmosphere of insecurity. There is for the faithful Christian the promise of a settled serenity in the peace which Jesus Christ can give.

(*b*) Some scholars think that what is here promised is fixity of moral character. In this life even the best of us is sometimes bad. But he who is faithful will in the end come to a time when he is like a pillar fixed in the Temple of God and goodness has become the constant atmosphere of his life. If this is the meaning, this phrase describes the life of untroubled goodness which is lived when, after the battles of earth, we reach the presence of God.

(iii) Jesus Christ will write upon the faithful Christian the name of his God. There may be three pictures here.

(*a*) In the cities of Asia Minor, and in Philadelphia, when a priest died after a lifetime of faithfulness, men honoured him, by erecting a new pillar in the temple in which he had served and by inscribing his name and the name of his father upon it.

This then would describe the lasting honour which Christ pays to his faithful ones.

(b) It is just possible that there is a reference to the custom of branding a slave with the initials of his owner to show that he belongs to him. Just so God will put his mark upon his faithful ones. Whichever picture is behind this, the sense is that the faithful ones will wear the unmistakable badge of God.

(c) It is just possible that we have an Old Testament picture. When God told to Moses the blessing which Aaron and the priests must pronounce over the people, he said: "They shall put my name upon the people of Israel" (*Numbers* 6: 22–27). It is the same idea again; it is as if the mark of God was upon Israel so that all men may know that they are his people.

(iv) On the faithful Christian the name of the new Jerusalem is to be written. That stands for the gift of citizenship in the city of God to the faithful Christian. According to Ezekiel the name of the re-created city of God was to be *The Lord is there* (*Ezekiel* 48: 35). The faithful ones will be citizens of the city where there is always the presence of God.

(v) On the faithful Christian Christ will write his own new name. The people of Philadelphia knew all about taking a new name. When in A.D. 17 a terrible earthquake devastated their city and Tiberius, the Emperor, dealt kindly with them, remitting taxation and making a generous gift to rebuild it, they in their gratitude, called the city Neocaesarea, the New City of Caesar, and later when Vespasian was kind to them, they called it Flavia, for that was the family name of Vespasian. Jesus Christ will mark his faithful ones with his new name: what that name was we need not even speculate, for no man knows it (*Revelation* 19: 12), but in the time to come, when Christ has conquered all, his faithful ones will bear the badge which shows that they are his and share his triumph.

THE LETTER TO LAODICEA

Revelation 3: 14–22

And to the angel of the Church in Laodicea, write:

These things says the Amen, the witness on whom you can rely and who is true, the moving cause of the creation of God.

I know your works; I know that you are neither cold nor hot. Would that you were cold or hot! So, because you are tepid and neither cold nor hot, I will vomit you out of my mouth. Because you say, I am rich and I have acquired riches, and I need nothing, and are quite unaware that it is you who are the wretched and the pitiable one, the poor and the blind and the naked one, I advise you to buy from me gold that has been refined by fire that you may be rich, white raiment that you may be clothed and that the shame of your nakedness may not be openly displayed, and eye-salve to anoint your eyes, that you may see.

I rebuke and discipline all those whom I love. Be eager, therefore, and repent.

Behold, I am standing at the door and knocking. If anyone hears my voice and opens the door, I will come in and will have my meal with him, and he with me.

I will give to him who overcomes to sit with me in my throne, even as I also overcame and took my seat with my Father in his throne.

Let him who has an ear hear what the Spirit is saying to the Churches.

LAODICEA
THE CHURCH CONDEMNED

Revelation 3: 14–22

LAODICEA has the grim distinction of being the only Church of which the Risen Christ has nothing good to say.

In the ancient world there were at least six cities called Laodicea and this one was called Laodicea on the Lycus to distinguish it from the others. It was founded about 250 B.C. by Antiochus of Syria and was named after his wife Laodicē.

Its importance was due entirely to its position. The road from Ephesus to the east and to Syria was the most important in Asia. It began at the coast at Ephesus and it had to find a way to climb up to the central plateau 8,500 feet up. It set out along the valley of the River Maeander until it reached what were known as the Gates of Phrygia. Beyond this point lay a broad valley where Lydia, Phrygia and Caria met. The Maeander entered that valley by a narrow, precipitous gorge through which no road could pass. The road, therefore, detoured through the Lycus valley. In that valley Laodicea stood.

It was literally astride the great road to the east which went straight through Laodicea, entering by the Ephesian Gate and leaving by the Syrian Gate. That in itself would have been enough to make Laodicea one of the great commercial and strategic centres of the ancient world. Originally Laodicea had been a fortress; but it had the serious handicap that all its water supply had to come by underground aqueduct from springs no less than six miles away, a perilous situation for a town besieged. Two other roads passed through the gates of Laodicea, that from Pergamum and the Hermus Valley to Pisidia and Pamphylia and the coast at Perga and that from eastern Caria to central and west Phrygia.

As Ramsay says: "It only needed peace to make Laodicea a great commercial and financial centre." That peace came with the dominion of Rome. When the Roman peace gave it its opportunity it became, as Pliny called it, "a most distinguished city."

Laodicea had certain characteristics which have left their mark on the letter written to it.

(i) It was a great banking and financial centre. When Cicero was travelling in Asia Minor it was at Laodicea that he cashed his letters of credit. It was one of the wealthiest cities in the world. In A.D. 61 it was devastated by an earthquake; but so rich and independent were its citizens that they refused any help from the Roman government and out of their own resources rebuilt their city. Tacitus writes: "One of the most famous cities of Asia, Laodicea, was in that same year overthrown by an earthquake and without any relief from us recovered itself by its own resources" (Tacitus: *Annals* 14: 27). No wonder that Laodicea could boast that it was rich and had amassed wealth and had need of nothing. It was so wealthy that it did not even need God.

(ii) It was a great centre of clothing manufacture. The sheep which grazed round Laodicea were famous for their soft, violet-black, glossy wool. It mass-produced cheap outer garments. It was specially connected with a tunic called the *trimita,* so much so, indeed, that it was sometimes called Trimitaria. Laodicea was so proud of the garments it produced that it never realized it was naked in the sight of God.

(iii) It was a very considerable medical centre. Thirteen miles to the west, between Laodicea and the Gate of Phrygia, stood the temple of the Carian god Men. At one time that temple was the social. administrative and commercial centre of the whole area. Until less than a hundred years ago great markets were regularly held on its site. In particular the temple was the centre of a medical school which was transferred to Laodicea itself. So famous were its doctors that the names of some appear on the coins of Laodicea. Two of them were called Zeuxis and Alexander Philalethes.

This medical school was famous for two things throughout the world, ointment for the ear and ointment for the eyes. The Authorized and Revised Standard Versions speak of eye-*salve.* The word for *salve* is *kollurion* which literally means *a little roll of bread.* The reason for the word is that this famous *tephra Phrygia,* Phrygian powder, was exported all over the world in solidified tablet form in the shape of little rolls. Laodicea was so conscious of its medical skill in the care of the eyes that it never realized that it was spiritually blind.

The words of the Risen Christ arise directly from the prosperity and the skill in which Laodicea took so much pride and which had in the minds of its citizens, and even of its Church, eliminated the need for God.

(iv) We add a final fact about Laodicea. It was in an area where there was a very large Jewish population. So many Jews emigrated here that the Rabbis inveighed against the Jews who sought the wines and baths of Phrygia. In 62 B.C. Flaccus, the governor of the province, became alarmed at the amount of currency which the Jews were exporting in payment of the Temple tax which every male Jew paid and put an embargo on the export of currency. The result was that twenty pounds weight of gold was seized as contraband in Laodicea and one hundred pounds in Apameia in Phrygia. That amount of gold would be equal to 15,000 silver *drachmae*. The Jewish Temple tax amounted to half a shekel, which was equal to two *drachmae*. This means that in the district there were at least 7,500 male Jews. In Hierapolis, six miles away from Laodicea, there was a "Congregation of Jews" which had power to levy and to retain fines, and an archive office where Jewish legal documents were specially kept. There can have been few areas where the Jews were wealthier and more influential.

LAODICEA
THE CLAIMS OF CHRIST

Revelation 3: 14–22 (*continued*)

OF all the seven Churches that of Laodicea is most unsparingly condemned. In it there is no redeemiing feature. It is interesting to note that the third century work *The Apostolic Constitutions* (8: 46) says that Archippus was the first Bishop of the Church in Laodicea. When Paul was writing to the neighbouring Church of Colossae, he says sternly: "Say to Archippus, See that you fulfil the ministry which you have received in the Lord" (*Colossians* 4: 17). It would seem that Archippus was somehow failing in his duty. That was thirty years before the *Revelation* was written; but it may be that as long ago as that the rot had set in in the Church in Laodicea and an unsatisfactory ministry had sown the seeds of degeneration.

Like all the letters it begins with a series of great titles of Jesus Christ.

(i) He is the Amen. This is a strange title and may go back to either of two origins.

(*a*) In *Isaiah* 65: 16 God is called the God of truth; but in the Hebrew he is called the *God of Amen*. Amen is the word which is often put at the end of a solemn statement in order to guarantee its truth. If God is the God of Amen, he is utterly to be relied upon. This would mean that Jesus Christ is the One whose promises are true beyond all doubt.

(*b*) In John's gospel Jesus's statements often begin: "Truly, truly, I say to you" (e.g. *John* 1: 51; 3: 3, 5, 11). The Greek for *truly* is *Amen*. It is possible that when Jesus Christ is called the Amen it is a reminiscence of his own way of speaking. The meaning would be the same, Jesus is one whose promises can be relied upon.

(ii) He is the witness on whom we can rely and who is true. Trench points out that a witness must satisfy three essential conditions. (*a*) He must have seen with his own eyes that of which he tells. (*b*) He must be absolutely honest, so that he repeats with accuracy that which he has heard and seen. (*c*) He must have the ability to tell what he has to say, so that his witness may make its true impression on those who hear. Jesus Christ perfectly satisfied these conditions. He can tell of God, because he came from him. We can rely on his words for he is the Amen. He is able to tell his message, for never did man speak as he did.

(iii) As the Revised Standard Version has it, he is the beginning of God's creation. This phrase, as it stands in English, is ambiguous. It could mean, either, that Jesus was the first person to be created or that he began the process of creation, as Trench put it, "dynamically the beginning." It is the second meaning which is intended here. The word for beginning is *archē*. In early Christian writings we read that Satan is the *archē* of death, that is to say, death takes its origin in him; and that God is the *archē* of all things, that is, all things find their beginning in him.

The connection of the Son with creation is frequently made in the New Testament. John begins his gospel by saying of the Word: "All things were made through him, and without him was not anything made that was made" (*John* 1: 3). "In him," says Paul, "all things were created" (*Colossians* 1: 15, 18). The insistence on the Son's part in creation was due to the heretics who explained sin and disease by saying that the world had been created by a false and inferior god. It is the Christian insistence that this world is God's creation and that its sin and sorrow are not his fault, but are caused by the disobedience of men. As the Christian sees it, the God of creation and the God of redemption are one and the same.

LAODICEA
NEITHER ONE THING NOR ANOTHER

Revelation 3: 14–22 (*continued*)

THE condemnation of Laodicea begins with a picture of almost crude vividness; because the Laodiceans are neither cold nor hot, they have about them a kind of nauseating quality, which will make the Risen Christ vomit them out of his mouth.

The exact meaning of the words is to be noted. *Cold* is *psuchros*; and it can mean cold to the point of freezing. *Ecclesiasticus* (43: 20) speaks of the *cold* north wind which makes the ice congeal upon the waters. *Hot* is *zestos*; and it means hot to boiling point. *Tepid* is *chliaros*. Things which are tepid often have a nauseating effect. Hot food and cold food can both be appetising, but tepid food will often make the stomach turn. Directly opposite Laodicea, on the other bank of the Lycus, and in full view, stood Hierapolis, famous for its hot mineral springs. Often hot mineral springs are nauseating in their taste and make the person who drinks them want to be physically sick. That is the way in which the Church at Laodicea affected the Risen Christ. Here is something to make us think:

(i) The one attitude which the Risen Christ unsparingly condemns is indifference. It has been said that an author can write a good biography if he loves his subject or hates him but not if he is coldly indifferent. Of all things indifference is the hardest to combat. The problem of modern evangelism is not hostility to Christianity; it would be better if it were so. The problem is that to so many Christianity and the Church have ceased to have any relevance and men regard them with complete indifference. This indifference can be broken down only by the actual demonstration that Christianity is a power to make life strong and a grace to make life beautiful.

(ii) The one impossible attitude to Christianity is neutrality. Jesus Christ works through men; and the man who remains completely detached in his attitude to him has by that very fact refused to undertake the work which is the divine purpose for him. The man who will not submit to Christ has necessarily resisted him.

(iii) Hard as it may sound, the meaning of this terrible threat of the Risen Christ is that it is better not even to start on the Christian way than to start and then to drift into a conventional and meaningless Christianity. The fire must be kept burning. There is an unwritten saying of Jesus: "He who is near me is near the fire." And the way to "maintain the spiritual glow" (*Romans* 12: 11, Moffat) is to live close to Christ.

LAODICEA
THE WEALTH THAT IS POVERTY

Revelation 3: 14–22 (*continued*)

THE tragedy of Laodicea was that it was convinced of its

own wealth and blind to its own poverty. Humanly speaking, anyone would say that there was not a more prosperous town in Asia Minor. Spiritually speaking, the Risen Christ declares that there was not a more poverty-stricken community. Laodicea prided itself on three things; and each is taken in turn and shown at its true value.

(i) It prided itself on its financial wealth. It was rich and had acquired wealth and had need of nothing—so it thought. The Risen Christ advises Laodicea to buy gold refined in the fire. It may be that gold tried in the fire stands for faith for it is thus that Peter describes faith (1 *Peter* 1: 7). Wealth can do much but there are things that it can never do. It cannot buy happiness nor give a man health either of body or of mind; it cannot bring comfort in sorrow nor fellowship in loneliness. If all that a man has to meet life with is wealth, he is poor indeed. But if a man has a faith tried and refined in the crucible of experience, there is nothing which he cannot face; and he is rich indeed.

(ii) Laodicea prided itself on its clothing trade. The garments made there were famous over all the world, and the wool of the sheep of Laodicea was a luxury article which all men knew. But, says the Risen Christ, Laodicea is spiritually naked; if it wants really to be clothed it must come to him. The Risen Christ speaks of "the shame of the nakedness of Laodicea."

This would mean even more in the ancient world than now. In the ancient world to be stripped naked was the worst humiliation. It was thus that Hanum treated the servants of David (2 *Samuel* 10: 4). The threat to Egypt is that Assyria will lead her people naked and barefoot (*Isaiah* 20: 4). It was Ezekiel's threat to Israel that her enemies would strip her of her clothes (*Ezekiel* 16: 37–39; 23: 26–29; cp. *Hosea* 2: 3, 9; *Micah* 1: 8, 11). God's threat passed on by Nahum to the disobedient people was: "I will let nations look on your nakedness, and on your kingdoms shame" (*Nahum* 3: 5). On the other hand, to be clothed in fine raiment was the greatest honour. Pharoah honoured Joseph by clothing him in vestures of fine linen (*Genesis* 41: 42). Daniel is clothed in purple by

Belshazzar (*Daniel* 5: 29). The royal apparel is for the man whom the king honours (*Esther* 6: 6–11). When the prodigal son returns, it is the best robe that is put upon him (*Luke* 15: 22).

Laodicea prides itself on the magnificent garments it produces but spiritually it is naked and nakedness is shame. The Risen Christ urges it to buy white raiment from him. This may well stand for the beauties of life and character which only the grace of Christ can give. There is little point in a man adorning his body, if he has nothing to adorn his soul. Not all the clothes in the world will beautify a person whose nature is twisted and whose character is ugly.

(iii) Laodicea prided itself on its famous eye-salve; but the facts of the case show that it was blind to its own poverty and nakedness. Trench says: "The beginning of all true amendment is to see ourselves as we are." All eye-salves in the ancient world caused the eyes to smart at their first application, and Laodicea had no wish to see itself as it was.

LAODICEA
LOVE'S CHASTISEMENT

Revelation 3: 14–22 (*continued*)

Verse 19 is one whose teaching runs throughout Scripture. "I rebuke and discipline all those whom I love." There is a very lovely thing about the way this is put. It is a quotation from *Proverbs* 3: 12, but one word is altered. In the Greek of the Septuagint the word for *love* is *agapan* which indicates the unconquerable attitude of goodwill which nothing can turn to hate; but it is a word which maybe has more of the head than the heart in it; and in the quotation the Risen Christ changes *agapan* to *philein* which is the most tender affection. We might well paraphrase it: "It is the people who are dearest to me on whom I exercise the sternest discipline."

Let us first take the word *rebuke*. The Greek is *elegchein* and it describes the kind of rebuke which compels a man to see the error of his ways. *Elegchos* is the corresponding noun, and Aristotle defines it: "*Elegchos* is the proof that a thing cannot be otherwise than we say." The most vivid example of this kind of rebuke is the way in which Nathan opened David's eyes to his sin (2 *Samuel* 12: 1–14). The rebuke of God is not so much punishment as illumination.

Let us see how the idea of discipline runs through the Bible.

It is very characteristic of the teaching of *Proverbs*. "He who spares the rod hates his son, but he who loves him is diligent to discipline him" (*Proverbs* 13: 24). "Withhold not correction from the child; for, if you beat him with a rod he will not die. If you beat him with the rod you will save his life from Sheol" (*Proverbs* 23: 13, 14). "Faithful are the wounds of a friend" (*Proverbs* 27: 6). "The rod and reproof give wisdom; but a child left to himself brings shame to his mother. . . . Discipline your son and he will give you rest; he will give delight to your heart" (*Proverbs* 29: 15, 17). "Blessed is the man whom thou dost chasten, O Lord, and whom thou dost teach out of thy law" (*Psalm* 94: 12). "Behold, happy is the man whom God reproves; therefore, despise not the chastening of the Almighty" (*Job* 5: 17). "We are chastened of the Lord that we may not be condemned along with the world" (1 *Corinthians* 11: 32). "For the Lord disciplines him whom he loves and chastises every son whom he receives. It is for discipline that you have to endure. God is testing you as sons; for what son is there whom his father does not discipline? If you are left without discipline, in which all have participated, then you are illegitimate children and not sons" (*Hebrews* 11: 6, 8). "He that loveth his son will continue to lay stripes upon him, that he may have joy of him in the end. He that chastiseth his son shall have profit of him and shall glory of him among his acquaintances" (*Ecclesiasticus* 30: 1).

It is, in fact, God's final punishment to leave a man alone. "Ephraim is joined to idols; let him alone" (*Hosea* 4: 17). As Trench has it: "The great Master-builder squares and polishes with many strokes of the chisel and hammer the stones

which shall find a place at last in the walls of the heavenly
Jerusalem. . . . It is the crushed grape, and not the untouched,
from which the costly liquor distils." There is no surer way
of allowing a child to end in ruin than to allow him to do
as he likes. It is a fact of life that the best athlete and the
finest scholar receive the most demanding training. The discipline of God is not something which we should resent, but
something for which we should be devoutly thankful.

LAODICEA
THE CHRIST WHO KNOCKS

Revelation 3: 14–22 (*continued*)

IN verse 20 we have one of the most famous pictures of Jesus
in the whole New Testament. "Behold," says the Risen Christ,
"I am standing at the door and knocking." This picture has
been derived from two different sources.

(i) It has been taken as a warning that the end is near, and
that the Coming of Christ is at hand. The Christian must be
ready to open whenever he hears his Lord knocking (*Luke*
12: 36). When the signs come, the Christian will know that
the last time is near, even at the doors (*Mark* 13: 29;
Matthew 24: 33). The Christian must live well and live in love
because the judge is standing at the doors (*James* 5: 9). It is
true that the New Testament uses this picture to express the
imminence of the coming of Christ. If that is the picture here,
this phrase contains a warning and tells men to have a care,
for Jesus Christ the Judge and King is at the door.

(ii) We cannot say that that meaning is impossible and yet
it does not seem to fit the context, for the atmosphere of
the passage is not so much warning as love. It is much better
to take this saying of Christ as expressing the appeal of the
lover of the souls of men. The origin of the passage is much
more likely to be in *Solomon's Song* when the lover stands
at the door of his beloved and pleads with her to open.
"Hark! my beloved is knocking. Open to me, my sister, my

love, my dove, perfect one" (*Solomon's Song* 5: 2–6). Here is Christ the lover knocking at the door of the hearts of men. And in this picture we see certain great truths of the Christian religion.

(*a*) We see the pleading of Christ. He stands at the door of the human heart and knocks. The unique new fact that Christianity brought into this world is that God is the seeker of men. No other religion has the vision of a seeking God.

In his book *Out of Nazareth* Donald Baillie cites three witnesses to the uniqueness of this conception. Montefiore, the great Jewish scholar, said that the one thing which no Jewish prophet or Rabbi ever conceived of is the "conception of God actually going out in quest of sinful men, who were not seeking him, but who were turned away from him." The National Christian Council of Japan in a document found the distinctive difference of Christianity from all other religions in, "Man not seeking God, but God taking the initiative in seeking man." St. Bernard away back in the twelfth century used often to say to his monks that, "However early they might wake and rise for prayer in their chapel on a cold mid-winter morning, or even in the dead of night, they would always find God awake before them, waiting for them—nay, it was he who had awakened them to seek his face."

Here is the picture of Christ searching for sinful men who did not want him. Surely love can go no further than that.

(*b*) We see the offer of Christ. As the Authorized Version has it, "I will come in and sup with him." The word translated sup is *deipnein* and its corresponding noun is *deipnon*. The Greeks had three meals in the day. There was *akratisma*, breakfast, which was no more than a piece of dried bread dipped in wine. There was *ariston,* the midday meal. A man did not go home for it; it was simply a picnic snack eaten by the side of the pavement, or in some colonnade, or in the city square. There was *deipnon*; this was the evening meal; the main meal of the day; people lingered over it, for the day's work was done. It was the *deipnon* that Christ would share with the man who answered his knock, no hurried meal, but that where people lingered in fellowship. If a man will open the door, Jesus Christ will come in and linger long with him.

(iii) We see human responsibility. Christ knocks and a man can answer or refuse to answer. Christ does not break in; he must be invited in. Even on the Emmaus road, "He appeared to be going further" (*Luke* 24: 28). Holman Hunt was right when in his famous picture *The Light of the World* he painted the door of the human heart with no handle on the outside, for it can be opened only from within. As Trench has it: "Every man is lord of the house of his own heart; it is his fortress; he must open the gates of it," and he has "the mournful prerogative and privilege of refusing to open." The man who refuses to open is "blindly at strife with his own blessedness." He is a "miserable conqueror."

Christ pleads and offers; but it is all to no avail if a man will not open the door.

THIS MEANS YOU

Revelation 3: 14–22 (*continued*)

THE promise of the Risen Christ is that the victor will sit with him in his own victorious throne. We will get the picture right if we remember that the eastern throne was more like a couch than a single seat. The victor in life will share the throne of the victorious Christ.

Every letter finishes with the words: "Let him who has an ear hear what the Spirit is saying to the Churches." This saying does two things.

(i) It individualizes the message of the letters. It says to every man: "This means you." So often we listen to a message which comes through a preacher and apply it to everyone but ourselves. In our heart of hearts we believe that the stern words cannot possibly be meant for us and that the promises are too good to be true for us. This phrase says to every one of us: "All these things are meant for *you*."

(ii) It generalizes the message of the letters. It means that their message was not confined to the people in the seven Churches nineteen hundred years ago, but that through them the Spirit is speaking to every man in every generation. We have set these letters carefully against the local situations to which they were addressed; but their message is not local and temporary. It is eternal and in them the Spirit still speaks to us.

THE OPENING HEAVENS AND THE OPENING DOOR

Revelation 4: 1

After this I saw, and, behold, a door in heaven was standing open, and there came to me the voice that I had heard before, speaking to me like the sound of a trumpet, and the speaker said: "Come up here, and I will show you the events which must follow these things."

IN chapters 2 and 3 we saw the Risen Christ walking amidst his churches upon earth. Now the scene changes to the court of heaven.

A door was opened in heaven for the seer. There are two possibilities here. (*a*) It may be that he is thought of as already being in heaven, and the door is opening into still more holy parts of heaven. (*b*) It is much more likely that the door is from earth to heaven. Primitive Jewish thought conceived of the sky as a vast solid dome, set like a roof upon a square flat earth; and the idea here is that beyond the dome of the sky there is heaven, and a door is opened in that dome to give the seer entry into heaven.

In the early chapters of the *Revelation* there are three of the most important doors in life.

(i) There is *the door of opportunity*. "Behold," said the Risen Christ to the Church at Philadelphia, "I have set before you an open door" (*Revelation* 3: 8). That was the door of the glorious opportunity by which the message of the gospel could be taken to the regions beyond. God sets before every man his own door of opportunity.

(ii) There is *the door of the human heart*. "Behold," says the Risen Christ, "I stand at the door and knock (*Revelation* 3: 20). At the door of every heart there comes the knock of the nail-pierced hand, and a man may open or refuse to open.

(iii) There is *the door of revelation*. "I saw a door in heaven standing open," says the seer. God offers to every man the door which leads to the knowledge of God and of life eternal.

More than once the New Testament speaks of the heavens *being opened*; and it is of the greatest significance to see the object of that opening.

(i) There is the opening of the heavens for *vision*. "The heavens were opened and I saw visions of God" (*Ezekiel* 1: 1). God sends to those who seek him the vision of himself and of his truth.

(ii) There is the opening for *the descent of the Spirit*. When Jesus was baptized by John, he saw the heavens opened and the Spirit descending upon himself (*Mark* 1: 10). When a man's mind and soul seek upwards, the Spirit of God descends to meet them.

(iii) There is the opening for *the revelation of the glory of Christ*. It was the promise of Jesus to Nathanael that he would see the heaven open and the angels of God ascending and descending upon the Son of Man (*John* 1: 51). Some day the heavens will open to disclose the glory of Christ; and inevitably that day will bring joy to those who have loved him and amazement and fear to those who have despised him.

THE THRONE OF GOD

Revelation 4: 2, 3

Immediately, I fell under the influence of the Spirit; and, behold, a throne stood in heaven, and there was One seated on it. And he who was seated on the throne was like a jasper stone and a sardian to look at; and there was a rainbow circling round the throne, like an emerald to look at.

WHEN the seer entered the door into heaven, he fell into an ecstasy.

In heaven he saw a throne and God on the throne. The throne of God is a common Old Testament picture. The prophet said: "I saw the Lord sitting on his throne, and all the host of heaven standing beside him" (1 *Kings* 22: 19). The Psalmist has it: "God sits on his holy throne" (*Psalm* 47: 8). Isaiah saw the Lord "sitting upon a throne, high and lifted up" (*Isaiah* 6: 1). In the *Revelation* the throne of God is mentioned in every chapter except 2, 8, and 9. The throne of God stands for the majesty of God. When Handel was asked how he had come to write the *Messiah,* his answer was: "I saw the heavens opened and God upon his great white throne."

John saw One seated upon the throne. There is something very interesting here. John makes no attempt to describe God in any human shape. As Swete says, "He rigorously shuns anthropomorphic details." He describes God in "the flashing of gem-like colours," but he never mentions any kind of form. It is the Bible's way to see God in terms of light. The Pastorals describe God as "dwelling in the light that no man can approach unto" (1 *Timothy* 6: 16). And long before that the Psalmist had spoken of God who covers himself with light as a garment (*Psalm* 104: 2).

John sees his vision in terms of the lights which flash from precious stones. We do not know what exactly these stones were. The three names here are the jasper, the sardian and the emerald. One thing is certain; these were typical of the most precious stones. Plato mentions the three of them together as representative of precious stones (Plato, *Phaedo* 111 E). They were part of the rich array of the King of Tyre (*Ezekiel* 28: 13); they were among the precious stones on the breast-plate of the High Priest (*Exodus* 28: 17); and they were among the stones which were the foundation of the Holy City (*Revelation* 21: 19).

The *jasper* is nowadays a dull opaque stone, but in the ancient world it seems to have been a translucent rock crystal, through which the light would come with an almost unbearable scintillation. Some think that here it means a diamond, and this is not impossible. The *sardian*, so called because it was said to be found mainly near Sardis, was blood-red; it was a gem which was frequently used to have engravings incised on it and may correspond to the modern carnelian. The *emerald* is most likely the green emerald which we know.

The picture of the presence of God which John saw was like the blinding flash of a diamond in the sun, with the dazzling blood-red of the sardian; and there flashed through both the more restful green of the emerald, for in that way alone could the eye bear to look upon the sight.

It may well be that the *jasper* stands for the unbearable brightness of the *purity* of God; that the blood-red *sardian* stands for his avenging *wrath*; and that the gentle green of the *emerald* stands for his *mercy* by which alone we can meet his purity and his justice.

THE TWENTY-FOUR ELDERS

Revelation 4: 4

> And in a circle round the throne I saw twenty-four thrones, and seated upon the thrones twenty-four elders, clothed in white garments, with golden crowns upon their heads.

WE now approach one of the difficult passages for which the *Revelation* is notorious. In it we meet twenty-four elders and then four living creatures; and we have to try to identify them.

We find the twenty-four elders frequently appearing in the *Revelation*. Let us set down the facts about them. They sit around the throne, clothed in white robes and wearing crowns (4: 4; 14: 3); they cast their crowns before the throne (4: 10); they continually worship and praise (5: 11, 14; 7: 11; 11: 16; 14: 3; 19: 4); they bring to God the prayers of the saints

(5: 8); one of them encourages the seer, when he is sad (5: 5); and one of them acts as interpreter of one of the visions (7: 13). We may note five lines of explanation.

(i) In the Old Testament there are indications of a kind of council surrounding God. The prophet sees God sitting on his throne and all the host of heaven standing by him on his right hand and on his left (1 *Kings* 22: 19). In *Job* the sons of God come to meet with him (*Job* 1: 6; 2: 1). Isaiah speaks of God reigning in glory among his elders (*Isaiah* 24: 23). In the *Genesis* story of the garden, the accusation against Adam is that he has eaten of the fruit of the forbidden tree and become like one of *us* (*Genesis* 3: 22). It may be that the idea of the elders has something to do with the idea of God's council surrounding him.

(ii) When the Jews were in Babylon, they could not avoid coming into contact with Babylonian ideas. And it might well be that sometimes they incorporated Babylonian ideas into their own thinking, especially if there was some initial resemblance. The Babylonians had twenty-four star gods, for the worship of the stars was a part of Babylonian religion; and it has been suggested that these became in Jewish thought twenty-four angels who surrounded the throne of God, and that the elders stand for these.

(iii) We move on to explanations which we think are much more likely. There were so many priests in Israel that they could not possibly serve in the Temple at the one time and so they were divided into twenty-four different courses (1 *Chronicles* 24: 7–18). Each of these courses had its president, known as an elder of the priests. Sometimes these elders were called princes, or governors, of the house of God (1 *Chronicles* 24: 5). It is suggested that the twenty-four elders stand symbolically for the twenty-four courses of the priests. They present the prayers of the faithful to God (*Revelation* 5: 8), and that is priestly work. The Levites were similarly divided into twenty-four courses for the work of the Temple and they praised God with harps and psalteries and cymbals (1 *Chronicles* 25: 6–31), and the elders also have their harps (*Revelation*

5: 8). So the twenty-four elders may stand for the heavenly ideal of the earthly worship of the priests and Levites in the Temple.

(iv) It has been suggested that the twenty-four elders stand for the twelve patriarchs and the twelve apostles combined. In the new Jerusalem the names of the twelve patriarchs are on the twelve gates and the names of the twelve apostles are on the foundation stones of the wall.

(v) We think that the likeliest explanation is that the twenty-four elders are the symbolic representatives of the faithful people of God. Their white robes are the robes promised to the faithful (*Revelation* 3: 4), and their crowns (*stephanoi)* are those promised to those who are faithful unto death (*Revelation* 2: 10). The thrones are those which Jesus promised to those who forsook all and followed him (*Matthew* 19: 27–29). The description of the twenty-four elders fits well with the promises made to the faithful.

The question will then be, "Why twenty-four?" The answer is because the Church is composed of Jews *and* Gentiles. There were originally twelve tribes, but now it is as if the tribes were doubled. Swete says that the twenty-four elders stand for the Church *in its totality*. We remember that this is a vision, not of what yet is, but of what shall be; and the twenty-four elders stand as representatives of the whole Church which one day in glory will worship in the presence of God himself.

AROUND THE THRONE

Revelation 4: 5, 6a

And flashes of lightning and voices and peals of thunder were coming forth from the throne. There were seven torches of fire burning before the throne, and these are the seven Spirits of God. And in front of the throne there was what I can only call a sea of glass like crystal.

JOHN adds more details to his mysterious and awe-inspiring picture of heaven. The voices are the voices of the thunder;

and thunder and lightning are often connected with the manifestation of God. In the vision of Ezekiel lightning comes out of the fiery haze around the throne (*Ezekiel* 1: 13). The Psalmist tells how the voice of the thunder of God was heard in the heavens, and the lightnings lightened the world (*Psalm* 77: 18). God sends his lightning to the ends of the earth (*Job* 37: 4). But what is primarily in the mind of John is the description of Mount Sinai as the people waited for the giving of the Law: "There were thunders and lightnings and a thick cloud upon the mountain, and a very loud trumpet blast" (*Exodus* 19: 16). John is using imagery which is regularly connected with the presence of God.

The seven torches are the seven Spirits of God. We have already met the seven Spirits before the throne (*Revelation* 1: 4; 3: 1). There are scholars who see Babylonian influence here also. For the Babylonians the seven planets were also divine and within the presence of God; it would be natural to liken the planets to torches and it has been suggested that this imagery is Babylonian in origin.

The "glassy sea" has exercised a strange fascination over the minds of many people, including hymn-writers. The Greek does not say that there was a sea of glass but "as it were a sea of glass." There was something which was beyond all description, but which could be likened only to a great sea of glass. Where did the seer get this picture?

(i) He may have got it from a conception in the most primitive thought of the Old Testament. We have already seen that the firmament is conceived of as a great solid dome arching over the earth. Beneath it is the earth, and above it the heaven. The creation story speaks of the waters under the firmament and the waters *above* the firmament (*Genesis* 1: 7). The Psalmist calls upon the waters that are above the heavens to praise the Lord (*Psalm* 148: 4). The belief was that above the firmament, perhaps as the kind of floor of heaven, there was a great sea. Further, it was on that sea that God had set his throne. The Psalmist says of God that he set the beams of his chambers upon the waters (*Psalm* 104: 3).

(ii) It may be that John's time in Patmos gave him the idea of this picture. Swete suggests that he saw a vast surface which flashed back the light, "like the Aegan Sea, when on summer days John looked upon it from the heights of Patmos." John had often seen the sea like a sea of molten glass and maybe his picture was born from that.

(iii) There is a further possibility. According to the *Koran* (Sura 27) Solomon had in his palace a floor of glass so like a sea that, when the Queen of Sheba came to visit him, she picked up her skirts thinking she had to wade through water. It may be that John is thinking of the throne of God set in a glass-floored palace.

(iv) There is one other remote possibility. John says that the glassy sea was like *crystal* (*krustallon*); but *krustallon* could mean *ice*; and then the idea would be an expanse which shimmered like an ice-field. It is a magnificent picture, but it can hardly be the real picture because neither John nor his people would ever have seen such a scene, and it would have meant nothing to them.

There are three things that this sea like shining glass does symbolize.

(i) It symbolizes *preciousness*. In the ancient world glass was usually dull and semi-opaque, and glass as clear as crystal was as precious as gold. In *Job* 28: 17 gold and glass are mentioned together as examples of precious things.

(ii) It symbolizes *dazzling purity*. The blinding light reflected from the glassy sea would be too much for the eyes to look upon, like the purity of God.

(iii) It symbolizes *immense distance*. The throne of God was in the immense distance, as if at the other side of a great sea. Swete writes of "the vast distance which, even in the case of one who stood in the door of heaven, intervened between himself and the throne of God."

One of the greatest characteristics of the writing of the seer is the reverence which, even in the heavenly places, never dares to be familiar with God, but paints its picture in terms of light and distance.

THE FOUR LIVING CREATURES (1)

Revelation 4: 6b–8

> And, between the throne and the elders, in a circle round the throne, were four living creatures, full of eyes in front and behind. The first living creature was like a lion; the second living creature was like an ox; the third living creature had what appeared to be a man's face; the fourth living creature was like an eagle in flight. The four living creatures had each of them six wings; and around and within they were full of eyes. Night and day they never rested from saying:
>
> Holy, holy, holy is the Lord, the Almighty, who was, and who is, and who is to come.

HERE we come to another of the symbolic problems of the *Revelation*. The four living creatures appear frequently in the heavenly scene: so let us begin by collecting what the *Revelation* itself says about them. They are always found near the throne and the Lamb (4: 6; 5: 6; 14: 4). They have six wings and they are full of eyes (4: 6, 8). They are constantly engaged in praising and in worshipping God (4: 8; 5: 9; 5: 14; 7: 11; 19: 4). They have certain functions to perform. They invite the dreadful manifestations of the wrath of God to appear upon the scene (6: 1; 6: 7). One of them hands over the vials of the wrath of God (15: 7).

Although there are definite differences, there can be little doubt that we find the ancestors of these living creatures in the visions of Ezekiel. In Ezekiel's vision the four living creatures each have four faces—the faces of a man, a lion, an ox and an eagle; and they uphold the firmament (*Ezekiel* 1: 6, 10, 22, 26); the felloes of the wheels are full of eyes (*Ezekiel* 1: 18). In *Ezekiel* we have all the details of the picture in the *Revelation,* although the details are differently allocated and arranged. In spite of the differences the family resemblance is clear.

In *Ezekiel* the four living creatures are definitely identified with the *cherubim.* (It is to be noted that *-im* is the Hebrew plural ending; *cherubim* is simply *cherubs* and *seraphim* is simply *seraphs*.) The identification is made in *Ezekiel* 10: 20, 22. The cherubim were part of the decoration of Solomon's Temple, in the place of prayer and on the walls (1 *Kings* 6: 23–30; 2 *Chronicles* 3: 7). They were represented on the hanging veil which shut off the Holy of Holies from the Holy Place (*Exodus* 26: 31). There were two cherubim on the lid of the ark, called the mercy-seat; and they were so placed that they faced each other and their wings swept over to form a kind of canopy over the mercy-seat (*Exodus* 25: 18–21). One of the commonest pictures of God is sitting between the cherubim, and it is thus that he is often addressed in prayer (2 *Kings* 19: 15; *Psalm* 80: 1; 99: 1; *Isaiah* 37: 16). God is represented as flying on the cherubim and on the wings of the wind (*Psalm* 18: 10). It is the cherubim who guard the way to the Garden when Adam and Eve have been banished from it (*Genesis* 3: 24). In the later books written between the Testaments, such as *Enoch*, the cherubim are the guardians of the throne of God (*Enoch* 71: 7).

From all this one thing emerges clearly—the cherubim are angelic beings who are close to God and the guardians of his throne.

THE FOUR LIVING CREATURES (2)

Revelation 4: 6b–8 (*continued*)

WHAT do these four living creatures symbolize?

(i) They are clearly part of the imagery of heaven; and they are not figures whom the writer of the *Revelation* did not create, but whom he inherited from previous pictures. They may originally have come from Babylonian sources, and they may have stood for the four principal signs of the Zodiac and for the four winds coming from the four quarters of heaven. But the John who wrote the *Revelation* was not aware of that, and he used them simply as part of the imagery of heaven in which he had been brought up.

(ii) How did John himself think of the symbolism of these

living creatures? We think that Swete offers the right explanation. The four living creatures stand for everything that is noblest, strongest, wisest and swiftest in nature. Each has the pre-eminence in his own particular sphere. The lion is supreme among beasts; the ox is supreme among cattle; the eagle is supreme among birds; and man is supreme among all creatures. The beasts represent all the greatness and the strength and the beauty of nature; here we see nature praising God. In the verses to follow we see the twenty-four elders praising God; and when we put the two pictures together we get the picture of both nature and man engaged in constant adoration of God. "The ceaseless activity of nature under the hand of God is a ceaseless tribute of praise."

The idea of nature praising God is one which occurs in the Old Testament more than once. "The heavens are telling the glory of God; and the firmament proclaims his handiwork. Day to day pours forth speech and night to night declares knowledge" (*Psalm* 19: 1, 2). "Bless the Lord all his works in all places of his dominion" (*Psalm* 103: 22). *Psalm* 148 is a magnificent summons to the whole of nature to join in praising God.

There is a tremendous truth here. The basic idea behind this is that anything which is fulfilling the function for which it was created is praising God. One of the basic conceptions of Stoicism was that in everything there was a spark of God, *scintilla*. "God," said Seneca, "is near you, with you, within you; a holy spirit sits within us." As Gilbert Murray points out, the sceptics laughed at this and sought to make a fool of the whole idea. "What," said the sceptic, "God in worms? God in dung beetles?" "Why not?" demanded the Stoic.

Cannot an earthworm serve God? Do you suppose that it is only a general who is a good soldier? Cannot the lowest private fight his best? Happy are you, if you are serving God and carrying out his purpose as faithfully as an earthworm. Whatever carries out the function for which it was created is thereby worshipping God.

This is a thought which opens out the most magnificent

vistas. The humblest and the most unseen activity in the world can be the true worship of God. Work and worship literally become one. Man's chief end is to glorify God and to enjoy him for ever; and man carries out that function when he does what God sent him into the world to do. Work well done rises like a hymn of praise to God.

This means that the doctor on his rounds, the scientist in his laboratory, the teacher in his classroom, the musician at his music, the artist at his canvas, the shop assistant at his counter, the typist at her typewriter, the housewife in her kitchen—all who are doing the work of the world as it should be done are joining in a great act of worship.

THE SYMBOLISM OF THE LIVING CREATURES

Revelation 4: 6b-8 (*continued*)

It was not long before the early church found certain symbolisms in the living creatures, in particular of the four Gospels—a representation which is often to be found in stained-glass windows in churches.

The earliest and the fullest identification was made by Irenaeus about A.D. 170. He held that the four living creatures represented four aspects of the work of Jesus Christ, which in turn are represented in the four Gospels.

The *lion* symbolizes the powerful and effective working of the Son of God, his leadership and his royal power. The *ox* signifies the priestly side of his work, for it is the animal of sacrifice. The *man* symbolizes his incarnation. The *eagle* represents the gift of the Holy Spirit, hovering with his wings over the Church. *John* represents "the original, effective and glorious generation of the Son from the Father," and tells how all things were made by him; and is, therefore, symbolized by the *lion*. *Luke* begins with the picture of Zacharias the priest, and tells the story of the fatted calf killed for the finding of the younger son; and is, therefore, symbolized by the *ox*. *Matthew* begins by giving us the human descent of Jesus and "The character of a humble and meek man is kept up throughout the whole gospel,"; and is, therefore, symbolized by the man. *Mark* begins with a reference to the Spirit of prophecy coming down from on high upon men which "points to the winged aspect of the Gospel,"; and, therefore, is symbolized by the *eagle*.

Irenaeus goes on to say that the fourfold form of the beasts represents the four principal covenants which God made with the human race. The first was made with Adam, prior to the flood. The second was made with Noah, after the flood. The third consisted of the giving of the Law to Moses. The fourth is that which renovates man in Christ, "raising and bearing men upon its wings into the heavenly kingdom."

But, as we have said, there was a variety of different identifications.

The scheme of Athanasius was:
Matthew = the man   Mark = the ox
Luke = the lion   John = the eagle.

The scheme of Victorinus was:
Matthew = the man   Mark = the lion
Luke = the ox   John = the eagle.

The scheme of Augustine was:
Matthew = the lion   Mark = the man
Luke = the ox   John = the eagle.

It may be said that on the whole Augustine's identifications became the most commonly accepted, because they fit the facts. *Matthew* is best represented by the *lion,* because in it Jesus is depicted as the Lion of Judah, the One in whom all the expectations of the prophets came true. *Mark* is best represented by the *man*, because it is the nearest approach to a factual report of the human life of Jesus. *Luke* is best represented by the *ox*, because it depicts Jesus as the sacrifice for all classes and conditions of men and women everywhere. *John* is best represented by the *eagle,* because of all birds it flies highest and is said to be the only living creature which can look straight into the sun; and *John* of all the gospels reaches the highest heights of thought.

THE SONG OF PRAISE

Revelation 4: 6b–8 (*continued*)

NIGHT and day the living creatures never rested from their doxology of praise:

> Holy, holy, holy is the Lord, the Almighty,
> Who was, and Who is, and Who is to come.

Here is set out the sleepless praise of nature. "Man rests on the Sabbath, and in sleep, and in the end in death, but the course of nature is unbroken and unbroken in praise." There is never any time when the world God made is not praising him.

> As o'er each continent and island
> The dawn leads on another day,
> The voice of prayer is never silent,
> Nor dies the strain of praise away.

The doxology seizes on three aspects of God.

(i) It praises him for *his holiness* (cp. *Isaiah* 6: 3). Again and again we have seen that the basic idea of holiness is difference. That is supremely true of God. He is different from men. Precisely there is the reason that we are moved to adoration of God. If he were simply a glorified human person, we could not praise. As the poet had it: "How could I praise, if such as I could understand?" The very mystery of God moves us to awed admiration in his presence and to amazed love that that greatness should stoop so low for us men and for our salvation.

(ii) It praises *his omnipotence*. God is the Almighty. The people to whom the *Revelation* was written are under the threat of the Roman Empire, a power which no person or nation had ever successfully withstood. Think what it must have meant to be sure that behind them stood the Almighty. The very giving of that name to God affirms the certainty of the safety of the Christian; not a safety which meant release from trouble but which made a man secure in life and in death.

(iii) It praises *his everlastingness*. Empires might come and empires might go; God lasts for ever. Here is the triumphant affirmation that God endures unchanging amidst the enmity and the rebellion of men.

GOD, THE LORD AND CREATOR

Revelation 4: 9–11

When the living creatures shall give glory and honour and thanksgiving to him who is seated on the throne and who lives for ever and ever, the twenty-four elders shall fall down before him who is seated on the throne, and worship him who lives for ever and ever, and cast their crowns before the throne, and say:

It is right, our Lord and God, that you should receive the glory and the honour and the power, for you have created all things, and through your will all things exist and have been created.

HERE is the other section of the choir of thanksgiving. We have seen that the living creatures stand for nature in all its greatness and the twenty-four elders for the great united Church in Jesus Christ. So when the living creatures and the elders unite in praise, it symbolizes nature and the Church both praising God. There are commentators who have made difficulty here. In verse 8 the praise of the living creatures is unceasing by day and night; in this passage the picture is of separate bursts of praise at each of which the elders fall down and worship. But surely to say that there is an inconsistency is unimaginative criticism; we do not look for a strict logic in the poetry of adoration.

John uses a picture which the ancient world would know well. The elders cast their crowns before the throne of God. In the ancient world that was the sign of complete submission. When one king surrendered to another, he cast his crown at the victor's feet. Sometimes the Romans carried with them an image of their emperor and, when they had reduced a monarch to submission, there was a ceremony in which the vanquished one had to cast his crown before the emperor's image. The picture looks on God as the conqueror of the souls of men; and on the Church as the body of people who have surrendered to him. There can be no Christianity without submission.

The doxology of the elders praises God on two counts.

(i) He is Lord and God. Here is something which would be even more meaningful to John's people than it is to us. The phrase for Lord and God is *kurios kai theos*; and that was the official title of Domitian, the Roman Emperor. It was, indeed, because the Christians would not acknowledge that claim that they were persecuted and killed. Simply to call God *Lord and God* was a triumphant confession of faith, an assertion that he holds first place in all the universe.

(ii) God is Creator. It is through his will and purpose that all things existed even before creation and were in the end brought into actual being. Man has acquired many powers, but he does not possess the power to create. He can alter and rearrange; he can make things out of already existing materials; but only God can create something out of nothing. That great truth means that in the realest sense everything in the world belongs to God, and there is nothing a man can handle which God has not given to him.

THE ROLL IN THE HAND OF GOD

Revelation 5: 1

> And in the right hand of him who was seated on the throne I saw a roll written on the front and on the back, and sealed with seven seals.

WE must try to visualize the picture which John is drawing. It is taken from the vision of Ezekiel: "And, when I looked, behold, a hand was stretched out to me; and lo, a written scroll was in it; and he spread it before me; and it had writing on the front and on the back; and there were written on it words of lamentation and mourning and woe" (*Ezekiel* 2: 9, 10).

We must note that it was a *roll* and not a *book* which was in the hand of God. In the ancient world, down to the second century A.D., the form of literary work was the roll, not the book. The roll was made of papyrus, manufactured in single sheets about ten inches by eight. The sheets were joined together horizontally when a great deal of writing had to be done. The writing was in narrow columns about three inches long, with margins of about two and a half inches at the top and at the bottom, and with about three-quarters of an inch between the columns. The roll commonly had a wooden roller at each end. It was held in the left hand, unrolled with the right, and, as the reading went on, the part in the left hand was rolled up again. We may get some idea of the dimensions of a roll from the following statistics. *Second* and *Third John, Jude* and *Philemon* would occupy one sheet of papyrus; *Romans* would require a roll 11½ feet long; *Mark,* 19 feet; *John,* 23½ feet; *Matthew,* 30 feet; *Luke* and *Acts,* 32 feet. The *Revelation* itself would occupy a roll 15 feet long. It was such a roll that was in the hand of God. Two things are said about it.

(i) It was written *on the front and on the back.* Papyrus was a substance made from the pith of a bulrush which grew in the delta of the Nile. The bulrush was about fifteen feet high, with six feet of it below the water; and it was as thick as a man's wrist. The pith was extracted and cut into thin strips with a very sharp knife. A row of strips was laid vertically; on the top of them another row of strips was laid horizontally; the whole was then moistened with Nile water and glue and pressed together. The resulting substance was beaten with a mallet and then smoothed with pumice stone; and there emerged a substance not unlike brown paper.

From this description it will be seen that on one side the grain of the papyrus would run horizontally; that side was known as the *recto*; and on that side the writing was done, as it was easier to write where the lines of the writing ran with the lines of the fibres. The side on which the fibres ran vertically was called the *verso* and was not so commonly used for writing.

But papyrus was an expensive substance. So, if a person had a great deal to write, he wrote both on the front and on the back. A sheet written on the back, the *verso,* was called an *opisthograph,* that is, a sheet written behind. Juvenal talks of a young tragedian walking about with the papyrus manuscript of a tragedy on Orestes written on both sides; it was a lengthy production! The roll in God's hand was written on both sides; there was so much on it that *recto* and *verso* alike were taken up with the writing.

(ii) It was *sealed with seven seals.* That may indicate either of two things.

(*a*) When a roll was finished, it was fastened with threads and the threads were sealed at the knots. The one ordinary document sealed with seven seals was a will. Under Roman law the seven witnesses to a will sealed it with their seals, and it could only be opened when all seven, or their legal representatives, were present. The roll may be what we might describe as God's will, his final settlement of the affairs of the universe.

(*b*) It is more likely that the seven seals stand simply for profound secrecy. The contents of the roll are so secret that it is sealed with seven seals. The tomb of Jesus was sealed to keep it safe (*Matthew* 27: 66); the apocryphal Gospel of Peter says that it was sealed with seven seals. It was so sealed to make quite certain that no unauthorized person could possibly open it.

GOD'S BOOK OF DESTINY

Revelation 5: 2–4

And I saw a strong angel proclaiming in a great voice: "Who is good enough to open the roll, and to loosen its seals?" And there was no one in heaven, or on earth, or under the earth, who was able to open the roll or to look at it; and I was weeping sorely because there was no one who was found to be good enough to open the roll or to see it.

As John looked at God with the roll in his hand, there came a challenge from a strong angel. A strong angel appears again in 10:1 and 18:21. In this case the angel had to be strong so that the challenge of his voice might reach throughout the universe. His summons was that anyone worthy of the task should come forward and open the book.

There is no doubt that the book is the record of that which is to happen in the last times. That there was such a book is a common conception in Jewish thought. It is common in the *Book of Enoch*. Uriel the archangel says to Enoch in the heavenly places: "O Enoch, observe the writing of the heavenly tablets, and read what is written thereon, and mark every individual fact." Enoch goes on: "And I observed everything on the heavenly tablets, and read everything which was written thereon, and understood everything, and read the book of all the deeds of men and of all the children of flesh that will be upon the earth to the remotest generations" (1 *Enoch* 81:1, 2). In the same book Enoch has a vision of the Head of Days on the throne of his glory, "and the books of the living were opened before him" (1 *Enoch* 47:3). Enoch declares that he knows the mystery of the holy ones, because "the Lord showed me and informed me, and I have read in the heavenly tables" (1 *Enoch* 106:19). On these tables he saw the history of the generations still to come (1 *Enoch* 107:1). The idea is that God has a book in which the history of time to come is already written.

When we are seeking to interpret this idea, it is well to remember that it is vision and poetry. It would be a great mistake to take it too literally. It does not mean that everything is settled long ago and that we are in the grip of an inescapable fate. What it does mean is that God has a plan for the universe; and that the purpose of God will be in the end worked out.

> God is working his purpose out, as year succeeds to year:
> God is working his purpose out, and the time is drawing near—
> Nearer and nearer draws the time—the time that shall surely be,
> When the earth shall be filled with the glory of God, as the waters cover the sea.

In response to the challenge of the angel no one came forward; none was good enough to open the roll. And at this John in his vision fell to weeping sorely. There were two reasons for his tears.

(i) In 4: 1 the voice had made the promise to him: "I will show you what must take place after this." It now looked as if the promise had been frustrated.

(ii) There is a deeper reason for his sorrow. It seemed to him that there was no one in the whole universe to whom God could reveal his mysteries. Here, indeed, was a terrible thing. Long ago Amos had said: "Surely the Lord God does nothing, without revealing his secrets to his servants the prophets" (*Amos* 3: 7). But here was a world so far from God that there was none able to receive his message.

For John that problem was to be triumphantly solved in the emergence of the Lamb. But behind this problem lies a great and a challenging truth. God cannot deliver a message to men unless there be a man fit to receive it. Here is the very essence of the problem of communication. It is the problem of the teacher; he cannot teach truth which his scholars are unable to receive. It is the problem of the preacher; he cannot deliver a message to a congregation totally incapable of comprehending it. It is the eternal problem of love; love cannot tell its truths or give its gifts to those incapable of hearing and receiving. The need of the world is for men and women who will keep themselves sensitive to God. He has a message for the world in every generation; but that message cannot be delivered until there is found a man capable of receiving it. And day by day we either fit or unfit ourselves to receive the message of God.

THE LION OF JUDAH AND THE ROOT OF DAVID

Revelation 5: 5

And one of the elders said to me: "Stop weeping. Behold the Lion of the tribe of Judah, the Root of David, has won such a victory that he is able to open the book and its seven seals."

WE are now approaching one of the most dramatic moments in the *Revelation,* the emergence of the Lamb in the centre of the scene. Certain things lead up to it.

John has been weeping because there is none to whom God may reveal his secrets. There comes to him one of the elders, acting as the messenger of Christ and saying to him: "Weep not." These words were more than once on the lips of Jesus in the days of his flesh. That is what he said to the widow of Nain when she was mourning her dead son (*Luke* 7: 13); and to Jairus and his family when they were lamenting for their little girl (*Luke* 8: 52). The comforting voice of Christ is still speaking in the heavenly places.

Swete has an interesting comment on this. John was weeping and yet his tears were unnecessary. Human grief often springs from insufficient knowledge. If we had patience to wait and trust, we would see that God has his own solutions for the situations which bring us tears.

The elder tells John that Jesus Christ has won such a victory that he is able to open the book and to loosen the seals. That means three things. It means that because of his victory over death and all the powers of evil and because of his complete obedience to God he is able to *know* God's secrets; he is able to *reveal* God's secrets; and it is his privilege and duty to *control* the things which shall be. Because of what Jesus did, he is the Lord of truth and of history. He is called by two great titles.

(i) He is the *Lion of Judah.* This title goes back to Jacob's final blessing of his sons before his death. In that blessing he calls Judah "a lion's whelp" (*Genesis* 49: 9). If Judah himself is a lion's whelp, it is fitting to call the greatest member of the tribe of Judah *The Lion of Judah.* In the books written between the Testaments this became a messianic title. 2 *Esdras* speaks of the figure of a lion and says: "This is the Anointed One, that is, the Messiah" (2 *Esdras* 12: 31). The strength of the lion and his undoubted place as king of beasts make him a fitting emblem of the all-powerful Messiah whom the Jews awaited.

(ii) He is the *Root of David*. This title goes back to *Isaiah's* prophecy that there will come forth a shoot from the stump of Jesse and a root of Jesse who shall be an ensign to the people (*Isaiah* 11: 1, 10). Jesse was the father of David, and this means that Jesus Christ was the Son of David, the promised Messiah.

So, here we have two great titles which are particularly Jewish. They have their origin in the pictures of the coming Messiah; and they lay it down that Jesus Christ triumphantly performed the work of the Messiah and is, therefore, able to know and to reveal the secrets of God, and to preside over the working out of his purposes in the events of history.

THE LAMB

Revelation 5: 6

And I saw a Lamb standing in the midst of the throne and of the four living creatures, and in the midst of the elders. It still bore the marks of having been slain. It had seven horns and seven eyes, which are the seven Spirits of God despatched to all the earth.

HERE is the supreme moment of this vision—the emergence of the Lamb in the scene of heaven. It is possible to think of this scene in two ways. Either we may think of the four living creatures forming a circle around the throne and the twenty-four elders forming a wider circle with a larger circumference, with the Lamb standing between the inner circle of the four living creatures and the outer circle of the twenty-four elders; or, much more likely, the Lamb is the centre of the whole scene.

The Lamb is one of the great characteristic ideas of the *Revelation* in which Jesus Christ is so called no fewer than twenty-nine times. The word he uses for *Lamb* is not used of Jesus Christ anywhere else in the New Testament. John the Baptist pointed to him as the Lamb of God who takes away the sin of the world (*John* 1: 29, 36). Peter speaks of the precious blood of Christ, as of a lamb without blemish and without spot (1 *Peter* 1: 19). In *Isaiah* 53: 7, in the chapter so dear to Jesus and to the early Church, we read of the lamb brought to the slaughter. But in all these cases the word is *amnos*, whereas the word that the *Revelation* uses is *arnion*. This is the word that Jeremiah uses, when he says: "I was like a gentle *lamb* that is led to the slaughter" (*Jeremiah* 11: 19). By using *arnion* and using it so often, John wishes us to see that this is a new conception which he is bringing to men.

(i) The Lamb still bears the marks of having been slain. There we have the picture of the sacrifice of Christ, still visible in the heavenly places. Even in the heavenly places Jesus Christ is the one who loved us and gave himself for us.

(ii) There is another side to this. This same Lamb, with the marks of sacrifice still on it, is the Lamb with the seven horns and the seven eyes.

(*a*) The seven horns stand for omnipotence. In the Old Testament the horn stands for two things.

First, it stands for sheer *power*. In the blessing of Moses the horns of Joseph are like the horns of a wild ox and with them he will push the people together to the ends of the earth (*Deuteronomy* 33: 17). Zedekiah, the prophet, made iron horns as a sign of promised triumph over the Syrians (1 *Kings* 22: 11). The wicked is warned not to lift up his horn (*Psalm* 75: 4). Zechariah sees the vision of the four horns which stand for the nations who have scattered Israel (*Zechariah* 1: 18).

Second, it stands for *honour*. It is the confidence of the Psalmist that in the favour of God our horn shall be exalted (*Psalm* 89: 17). The good man's horn shall be exalted with honour (*Psalm* 112: 9). God exalts the horn of his people (*Psalm* 148: 14).

We must add still another strand to this picture. In the time between the Testaments the great heroes of Israel were the Maccabees; they were the great warriors who were the liberators of the nations; and they are represented as horned lambs (1 *Enoch* 90: 9).

Here is the great paradox; the Lamb bears the sacrificial wounds upon it; but at the same time it is clothed with the very might of God which can now shatter its enemies. The Lamb has *seven* horns; the number *seven* stands for perfection; the power of the Lamb is perfect, beyond withstanding.

(*b*) The Lamb has seven eyes, and the eyes are the Spirits which are despatched into all the earth. The picture comes from *Zechariah*. There the prophet sees the seven lamps which are "the eyes of the Lord, which range through the whole earth" (*Zechariah* 4: 10). It is an eerie picture; but quite clearly it stands for the omniscience of God. In an almost crude way it says that there is no place on earth which is not under the eye of God.

Here is a trememdous picture of Christ. He is the fulfilment of all the hopes and dreams of Israel, for he is the Lion of Judah and the Root of David. He is the one whose sacrifice availed for men, and who still bears the marks of it in the heavenly places. But the tragedy has turned to triumph and the shame to glory; and he is the one whose all-conquering might none can withstand and whose all-seeing eye none can escape.

Few passages of Scripture show at one and the same time what Swete called "the majesty and the meekness" of Jesus Christ and in the one picture combine the humiliation of his death and the glory of his risen life.

MUSIC IN HEAVEN

Revelation 5: 7-14

And the Lamb came and received the roll from the right hand of him who was seated on the throne. When it had received the roll, the four living creatures fell before the Lamb and so did the twenty-four elders, each of whom had a harp and golden bowls laden with incenses, which are the prayers of God's dedicated people. And they sang a new song and this is what they sang:

Worthy are you to receive the roll and to open its seals, because you were slain, and so at the price of your life blood you bought for God those of every tribe and tongue and people and race and made them a kingdom of priests to our God, and they will reign upon the earth.

And I saw, and I heard the voice of many angels, who were in a circle round the throne, and the living creatures, and the elders; and their number was ten thousands of ten thousands and thousands of thousands, and they were singing with a great voice:

The Lamb which has been slain is worthy to receive the power and the riches and the wisdom and the strength and the honour and the glory and the blessing.

And I heard every created creature which was in the heaven and upon the earth and beneath the earth and on the sea and all things in them saying:

Blessing and honour and glory and dominion for ever and ever to him who sits upon the throne and to the Lamb.

And the four living creatures said, Amen; and the elders fell down and worshipped.

IT is necessary to look at this passage as a whole before we begin to deal with it in detail. R. H. Charles quotes Christian Rossetti on it; "Heaven is revealed to earth as the homeland of music." Here is the greatest chorus of praise the universe can ever hear. It comes in three waves. First, there is the praise of the four living creatures and of the twenty-four elders. Here we see all nature and all the Church combining to praise the Lamb. Second, there is the praise of the myriads of angels. Here is the picture of all the inhabitants of heaven lifting up their voices in praise. Third, John sees every created creature, in every part of the universe, to its deepest depth and its farthest corner, singing in praise.

Here is the truth that heaven and earth and all that is within them is designed for the praise of Jesus Christ; and it is our privilege to lend our voices and our lives to this vast chorus of praise, for that chorus is necessarily incomplete so long as there is one voice missing from it.

THE PRAYERS OF THE SAINTS

Revelation 5: 8

THE first section in the chorus of praise is the song of the four living creatures and the twenty-four elders; and, as we have seen, they represent all that is in nature and in the universal Church.

The picture of the elders is interesting. They have harps. The harp was the traditional instrument to which the Psalms were sung. "Praise the Lord with harp," says the Psalmist (*Psalm* 33: 2). "Sing praises to the Lord with the harp; the harp, and the sound of melody" (*Psalm* 98: 5). "Sing to the Lord with thanksgiving; make melody to our God upon the harp" (*Psalm* 147: 7). The harp stands for the music of praise as the Jews knew it.

The elders also have golden bowls full of incense; and the incense is the prayers of God's dedicated people. The likening of prayers to incense comes also from the *Psalms*. "Let my prayer be before thee counted as incense; and the lifting up of my hands as an evening sacrifice" (*Psalm* 141: 2). But the significant thing is the idea of intermediaries in prayer. In later Jewish literature this idea of heavenly intermediaries bringing the prayers of the faithful to God is very common. In the *Testament of Dan* (6: 2) we read: "Draw near unto God and to the angel that intercedeth for you, for he is a mediator between God and man." In this literature we find many such angels.

Chief of them all is Michael, the archangel, "the merciful and long-suffering" (1 *Enoch* 40: 9). He is said daily to come down to the fifth heaven to receive men's prayers and to bring them to God (3 *Baruch* 11). In *Tobit* it is the archangel Raphael who brings the prayers of men to God; "I am Raphael, one of the seven holy angels, who present the prayers of the saints, and who go in and out before the glory of the Holy One" (*Tobit* 12: 15). It is Gabriel who tells Enoch: "I swear unto you that in heaven the angels are mindful of you before the glory of the Great One" (1 *Enoch* 104: 1). Sometimes it is the guardian angels who bring the prayers of men to God; and it is said that at certain times each day the doors are open so that the prayers may be received (*Apocalypse of Paul* 7: 10). Sometimes all the angels, or, as *Enoch* calls them, The Watchers, are engaged in this task. It is to "the Holy Ones of Heaven" that the souls of men complain with their cry for justice (1 *Enoch* 9: 3). It is the duty of the Watchers of heaven to intercede for men (1 *Enoch* 15: 2). As we have seen, the angels are mindful of men for good (1 *Enoch* 104: 1). Sometimes, it would seem, the blessed dead share in this task. The angels and the holy ones in their resting-places intercede for the children of men (1 *Enoch* 39: 6). There are certain things to be said about this belief in heavenly intermediaries.

(i) From one point of view it is an uplifting thought. We are, so to speak, not left to pray alone. No prayer can be altogether heavy-footed and leaden-winged which has all the citizenry of heaven behind it to help it rise to God.

(ii) From another point of view it is quite unnecessary. Before us is set an open door which no man can ever shut; no man's prayers need any assistance, for God's ear is open to catch the faintest whisper of appeal.

(iii) The whole conception of intermediaries arises from a line of thought which has met us before. As the centuries went on, the Jews became ever more impressed with the transcendence of God, his difference from men. They began to believe that there never could be any direct contact between God and man and that there must be angelic intermediaries to bridge the gulf. That is exactly the feeling that Jesus Christ came to take away; he came to tell us that God "is closer to us than breathing, nearer than hands or feet" and to be the living way by which for every man, however humble, the door to God is open.

THE NEW SONG

Revelation 5: 9

THE song that the four living creatures and the elders sang

was a *new song*. The phrase *a new song* is very common in the *Psalms*; and there it is always a song for the new mercies of God. "Sing to him a new song," says the Psalmist (*Psalm* 33: 3). God took the Psalmist out of the fearful pit and from the miry clay and set his foot on a rock and put a new song in his mouth to praise God (*Psalm* 40: 3). "O sing a new song to the Lord, for he has done marvellous things" (*Psalm* 98: 1; cp. 96: 1). "I will sing a new song to thee, O God" (*Psalm* 144: 9). "Praise the Lord. Sing to the Lord a new song, his praise in the assembly of the faithful" (*Psalm* 149: 1). The nearest parallel in the Old Testament comes from *Isaiah*. There God declares new things and the prophet calls upon men to sing to the Lord a new song (*Isaiah* 42: 9, 10).

The new song is always a song for new mercies of God; and it will be noblest of all when it is a song for the mercies of God in Jesus Christ.

One of the characteristics of the *Revelation* is that it is the book of new things. There is the new name (2: 17; 3: 12); there is the new Jerusalem (3: 12; 21: 2); there is the new song (5: 9; 14: 3); there are the new heavens and the new earth (21: 1); and there is the great promise that God makes all things new (21: 5).

One most significant thing is to be noted. Greek has two words for *new*, *neos*, which means *new in point of time* but not necessarily in point of quality, and *kainos,* which means *new in point of quality. Kainos* describes a thing which has not only been recently produced but whose like has never existed before.

The significance of this is that Jesus Christ brings into life a quality which has never existed before, new joy, new thrill, new strength, new peace. That is why the supreme quality of the Christian life is a kind of sheen. It has been said that "the opposite of a Christian world is a world grown old and sad."

THE SONG OF THE LIVING CREATURES AND OF THE ELDERS

Revelation 5: 9, 10

LET us begin by setting down this song:

> Worthy are you to receive the roll, and to open its seals, because you were slain, and so at the price of your life blood you bought for God those of every tribe and tongue and people and race, and made them a kingdom of priests to our God, and they will reign upon the earth.

The praise rendered to the Lamb by the four living creatures and the elders is rendered because he died. In this song there is summed up the results of the death of Jesus Christ.

(i) It was a *sacrificial* death. That is to say, it was a death with purpose in it. It was not an accident of history; it was not even the tragic death of a good and heroic man in the cause of righteousness and of God; it was a sacrificial death. The object of sacrifice is to restore the lost relationship between God and man; and it was for that purpose, *and with that result*, that Jesus Christ died.

(ii) The death of Jesus Christ was an *emancipating* death. From beginning to end the New Testament is full of the idea of the liberation of mankind achieved by him. He gave his life a ransom (*lutron*) for many (*Mark* 10: 45). He gave himself a ransom (*antilutron*) for all (1 *Timothy* 2: 6). He redeemed us—literally *bought us out from (exagorazein)*—from the curse of the law (*Galatians* 3: 13). We are redeemed (*lutrousthai*) not by any human wealth but by the precious blood of Jesus Christ (1 *Peter* 1: 19). Jesus Christ is the Lord that bought us (*agorazein*) (2 *Peter* 2: 1). We are bought with a price (*agorazein*) (1 *Corinthians* 6: 20; 7: 23). The New Testament consistently declares that it cost the death of Jesus Christ to rescue man from the dilemma and the slavery into which sin had brought him. The New Testament has no "official" theory of how that effect was achieved; but of the effect itself it is in no doubt whatever.

(iii) The death of Jesus Christ was *universal* in its benefits. It was for men and women of every race. There was a day when the Jews could hold that God cared only for them and wished for nothing but the destruction of other peoples. But in Jesus Christ we meet a God who loves *the world*. The death of Christ was for all men and, therefore, it is the task of the Church to tell all men of it.

(iv) The death of Jesus Christ was an *availing* death. He did not die for nothing. In this song three aspects of the work of Christ are singled out.

(*a*) He made us *kings*. He opened to men the royalty of sonship of God. Men have always been sons of God by creation; but now there is a new sonship of grace open to every man.

(*b*) He made us *priests*. In the ancient world the priest alone had the right of approach to God. When an ordinary Jew entered the Temple, he could make his way through the Court of the Gentiles, through the Court of the Women, into the Court of the Israelities; but into the Court of the Priests he could not go. It was thus far and no farther. But Jesus Christ opened the way for all men to God. Every man becomes a priest in the sense that he has the right of access to God.

(*c*) He gave us *triumph*. His people shall reign upon the earth. This is not political triumph or material lordship. It is the secret of victorious living under any circumstances. "In the world you have tribulation; but be of good cheer, I have overcome the world" (*John* 16: 33). In Christ there is victory over self, victory over circumstance and victory over sin.

When we think of what the death and life of Jesus Christ have done for men, it is no wonder that the living creatures and the elders burst into praise of him.

THE SONG OF THE ANGELS

Revelation 5: 11, 12

And I saw, and I heard the voice of many angels, who were in a circle round the throne and the living creatures and the elders; and their number was ten thousands of ten thousands and thousands of thousands; and they were saying with a great voice:

The Lamb, which has been slain, is worthy to receive the power and the riches and the wisdom and the strength and the honour and the glory and the blessing.

THE chorus of praise is taken up by the unnumbered hosts of the angels of heaven. They stand in a great outer circle round the throne and the living creatures and the elders and they begin their song. We have repeatedly seen how John takes his language from the Old Testament; and here there is in his memory David's great thanksgiving to God:

Blessed art thou, O Lord, the God of Israel, our Father, for ever and ever. Thine, O Lord, is the greatness and the power and the glory and the victory and the majesty; for all that is in the heavens and in the earth is thine; thine is the kingdom, O Lord, and thou art exalted as head above all. Both riches and honour come from thee, and thou rulest over all. In thy hand are power and might; and in thy hand it is to make great, and to give strength to all (*1 Chronicles* 29: 10–12).

The song of the living creatures and of the elders told of the work of Christ in his death; now the angels sing of the possessions of Christ in his glory. Seven great possessions belong to the Risen Lord.

(i) To him belongs the *power*. Paul called Jesus, "Christ the power of God" (1 *Corinthians* 1: 24). He is not one who can plan but never achieve; to him belongs the power. We can say triumphantly of him: "He is able."

(ii) To him belongs the *riches*. "Though he was rich, yet for your sake he became poor" (2 *Corinthians* 8: 9). Paul speaks of "the unsearchable riches of Christ" (*Ephesians* 3: 8). There is no promise that Jesus Christ has made that he does not possess the resources to carry out. There is no claim on him which he cannot satisfy.

(iii) To him belongs the *wisdom*. Paul calls Jesus Christ "the wisdom of God" (1 *Corinthians* 1: 24). He has the wisdom

to know the secrets of God and the solution of the problems
of life.

(iv) To him belongs the *strength*. Christ is the strong one
who can disarm the powers of evil and overthrow Satan
(*Luke* 11:22). There is no situation with which he cannot cope.

(v) To him belongs the *honour*. The day comes when to
him every knee shall bow and every tongue shall confess that
he is Lord (*Philippians* 2:11). A strange thing is that even
those who are not Christian often honour Christ by admitting
that in his teaching alone lies the hope of this distracted world.

(vi) To him belongs the *glory*. As John has it: "We beheld
his glory, from glory as of the only Father, full of grace
and truth" (*John* 1:14). Glory is that which by right belongs
to God alone. To say that Jesus Christ possesses the glory
is to say that he is divine.

(vii) To him belongs the *blessing*. Here is the inevitable
climax of it all. All these things Jesus Christ possesses, and
every one of them he uses in the service of the men for
whom he lived and died; he does not clutch them to himself.

Therefore, there rises to him from all the redeemed thanksgiving for all that he has done. And that thanksgiving is the
one gift that we who have nothing can give to him who
possesses all.

THE SONG OF ALL CREATION

Revelation 5:13, 14

> And I heard every created creature which was in the heaven, and
> upon the earth, and beneath the earth, and on the sea, and all
> things in them, saying:
>> Blessing and honour and glory and dominion for ever and ever
>> to him who sits upon the throne and to the Lamb.
> And the four living creatures said, Amen; and the elders fell down
> and worshipped.

Now the chorus of praise goes so far that it cannot go farther, for it reaches throughout the whole of the universe and the whole of creation. There is one vast song of praise to the Lamb. We may note one very significant thing. In this chorus of praise God and the Lamb are joined together. Nothing could better show the height of John's conception of Jesus Christ. In the praise of creation he sets him by the side of God.

In the song itself there are two things to note.

The creatures which are in the heaven add their praise. Who are they? More than one answer has been given and each is lovely in its own way. It has been suggested that the reference is to the birds of the air; the very singing of the birds is a song of praise. It has been suggested that the reference is to the sun, the moon and the stars; the heavenly bodies in their shining are praising God. It has been suggested that the phrase gathers up every possible being in heaven—the living creatures, the elders, the myriads of angels and every other heavenly being.

The creatures which are beneath the earth add their praise. That can only mean the dead who are in Hades, and here is something totally new. In the Old Testament the idea is that the dead are separated altogether from God and man and live a shadowy existence. "In death there is no rememberence of thee; in Sheol who can give thee praise?" (*Psalm* 6: 5). "Shall the dust praise thee? Shall it declare thy truth? What profit is there in my death if I go down to the pit?" (*Psalm* 30: 9). "Dost thou work wonders for the dead? Do the shades rise up to praise thee? Is thy steadfast love declared in the grave, or thy faithfulness in Abaddon? Are thy wonders known in the darkness, or thy saving help in the land of forgetfulness?" (*Psalm* 88: 10–12). "For Sheol cannot thank thee, death cannot praise thee; those that go down to the pit cannot hope for thy faithfulness" (*Isaiah* 38: 18).

Here is a vision which sweeps all this away. Not even the land of the dead is beyond the reign of the Risen Christ. Even from beyond death the chorus of praise rises to him.

The picture here is all-inclusive of all nature praising God.

There are in Scripture many magnificent pictures of the praise
of God by nature. In the Old Testament itself there is *Psalm*
148. But the noblest song of praise comes from the Apocrypha.
In the Greek Old Testament there is an addition to *Daniel*. It
is called *The Song of the Three Children* and it is sung by
Ananias, Azarias, and Misael, as Shadrach, Meshach and
Abed-nego are there called, before they enter the fiery furnace.
It is long, but it is one of the world's great poems, and we must
quote in full the part in which they call upon nature to praise
God.

O ye sun and moon, bless ye the Lord:
Praise and exalt him above all for ever.
O ye stars of heaven, bless ye the Lord:
Praise and exalt him above all for ever.
O every shower and dew, bless ye the Lord:
Praise and exalt him above all for ever.
O all ye winds, bless ye the Lord:
Praise and exalt him above all for ever.
O ye fire and heat, bless ye the Lord:
Praise and exalt him above all for ever.
O ye winter and summer, bless the Lord:
Praise and exalt him above all for ever.
O ye dews and storms of snow, bless ye the Lord:
Praise and exalt him above all for ever.
O ye nights and days, bless the Lord:
Praise and exalt him above all for ever.
O ye light and darkness, bless the Lord:
Praise and exalt him above all for ever.
O ye cold and heat, bless the Lord:
Praise and exalt him above all for ever.
O ye ice and cold, bless ye the Lord:
Praise and exalt him above all for ever.
O ye frost and snow, bless ye the Lord:
Praise and exalt him above all for ever.
O ye lightnings and clouds, bless ye the Lord:
Praise and exalt him above all for ever.
O let the earth bless the Lord:
Praise and exalt him above all for ever.
O ye mountains and little hills, bless ye the Lord:
Praise and exalt him above all for ever.

O all ye herbs of the field, bless ye the Lord:
Praise and exalt him above all for ever.
O all things that grow on the earth, bless ye the Lord:
Praise and exalt him above all for ever.
O ye fountains, bless ye the Lord:
Praise and exalt him above all for ever.
O ye seas and rivers, bless ye the Lord:
Praise and exalt him above all for ever.
O ye whales and all that move in the waters, bless ye the
    Lord:
Praise and exalt him above all for ever.
O all ye fowls of the air, bless ye the Lord:
Praise and exalt him above all for ever.
O all ye beasts and cattle, bless ye the Lord:
Praise and exalt him above all for ever.
O all ye creeping things of the earth, bless ye the Lord:
Praise and exalt him above all for ever.
O ye children of men, bless ye the Lord:
Praise and exalt him above all for ever.

FURTHER READING

G. B. Caird, *The Revelation of Saint John the Divine* (ACB; *E*)
R. H. Charles, *Revelation* (ICC; *G*)
T. S. Kepler, *The Book of Revelation*
H. B. Swete, *The Apocalypse of St John* (MmC; *G*)

Abbreviations

ACB : A. and C. Black New Testament Commentary
ICC : International Critical Commentary
MmC: Macmillan Commentary

E : English Text
G : Greek Text